MOB
DAUGHTER

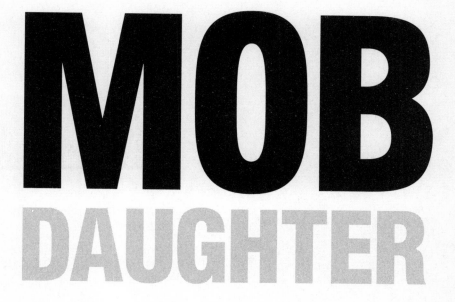

MOB
DAUGHTER

THE MAFIA, SAMMY "THE BULL" GRAVANO, AND ME!

KAREN GRAVANO
WITH LISA PULITZER

ST. MARTIN'S PRESS ⚌ NEW YORK

MOB DAUGHTER.

Copyright © 2012 by Karen Gravano with Lisa Pulitzer.

All rights reserved. Printed in the United States of America. For information, address St. Martin's Press, 175 Fifth Avenue, New York, N.Y. 10010.

Photo on pp. ii–iii courtesy of Sandra Scibetta.

www.stmartins.com

Design by Anna Gorovoy

Library of Congress Cataloging-in-Publication Data

Gravano, Karen.

  Mob daughter : the Mafia, Sammy "The Bull" Gravano, and me! / Karen Gravano with Lisa Pulitzer.—1st ed.

      p. cm.

  ISBN 978-1-250-00305-8 (hardcover)

  ISBN 978-1-250-01520-4 (e-book)

  1. Gravano, Karen.   2. Gravano, Salvatore, 1945—Family.   3. Mafia—New York (State)—New York.   4. Children of criminals—Family relationships—United States.   I. Pulitzer, Lisa.   II. Title.

  HV6248.G647G73 2012

  364.1092—dc23

  [B]   2011043170

First Edition: February 2012

10 9 8 7 6 5 4 3 2 1

ACKNOWLEDGMENTS

I'd like to acknowledge my special friends and family who have been in my corner and believed in me through all my ups and downs.

David, thanks for being a great father to our beautiful daughter Karina and for always being there when it counts.

Karina and Nicholas: you are the loves of my life. I am so proud of both of you.

Dad, Mom, and Gerard: you are my foundation and support team. Throughout everything we've been through in life we have always remained ONE. I am so proud to call each one of you family. I love you all.

To everyone from the offices to the field that works so hard every day to create *Mob Wives*, thanks for putting up with us.

To all the people that watch and support *Mob Wives*, you

ACKNOWLEDGMENTS

make the show worth doing. And to the people who have taken
the time to reach out to me personally, trust me, your support is
very much appreciated. And a special thanks to everyone who
helped this book come to life. Lisa, our hard work is complete.
xoxo

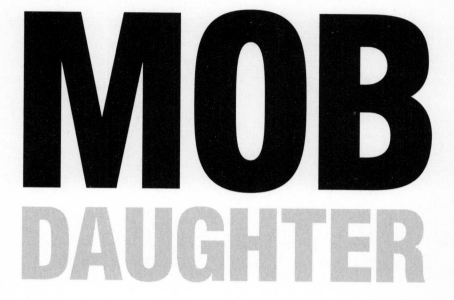

PROLOGUE

"God don't like that, Nick."

I could feel my stomach tightening as I steered the rental car toward the sprawling complex of dreary cement-block buildings. The prison where my father was being housed looked even more ominous than I imagined, isolated at the end of a narrow dirt road, sixty miles from the nearest town and surrounded by mountains and twelve-foot razor-wire fencing. My father had just been moved to this location after spending two years in solitary confinement at an undisclosed federal prison and five more at ADX outside Florence, Colorado. ADX, also known as the Alcatraz of the Rockies, is an all-male "supermax" prison that houses some of the country's most dangerous criminals, high-ranking mobsters, terrorists, and serial murderers.

It had been years since I'd last seen my dad, Sammy "the Bull" Gravano, in person. Our previous visit hadn't gone well.

We'd spent much of the time arguing. I was very strong-minded, just like my father, and we didn't always see eye to eye. I was hoping this wasn't going to be a repeat performance, especially since I had my mother, nine-year-old daughter, Karina, and ten-year-old nephew, Nicholas, along.

When my father was incarcerated at ADX, it had been hard communicating with him by phone. He'd been in solitary confinement for seven long years and had been allowed to make only one fifteen-minute call a month. If I was not home to answer, he would have to wait another month to try again. On the rare occasions that we did connect, he was frustrated and angry. For five years, he'd been on twenty-three-hour-a-day lockdown, and other than his monthly phone call to the family, had been permitted no contact with the outside world. He showered and ate all of his meals in his four-by-six-foot cell, located in a wing where the lights were kept on twenty-four hours a day. Every cell had a surveillance camera in it.

The only person to have visited him at ADX Florence was my mother. She told me that he had been transported to the visiting area in a cage with wheels just like Hannibal Lecter in the movie *The Silence of the Lambs*. They'd been holding him in a special unit for high-profile inmates. There could be no physical contact, not even handholding. She had to talk to him through the bullet-proof poleax glass. They wouldn't even remove his shackles during her visit.

The years of lockdown and lack of socialization had taken their toll. Once while at ADX he called me and started telling me about the bugs that visited him in his cell in the evenings, which freaked me out. He joked that they were his "friends." He'd even named them because he was so bored. I had nightmares for months. He didn't want anyone to visit him and said to stay in touch by mail.

My father had finally gotten out of solitary confinement, and was sounding a lot less angry and more like the man I remembered from my childhood. He had felt useless to his family in solitary, and that had been frustrating him. Talking to him on the phone had been bringing back memories of happier times and I'd started missing him. My father was not well, and I didn't know how much longer he'd be around. He was diagnosed with Graves' disease while in prison, a chronic thyroid condition affecting the immune system. I was concerned the illness was taking its toll. I was troubled by the poor medical attention he had been receiving and the fact that he had not been able to work out in a physical way as he once had done.

Because of his "high-profile" status as a Mafia boss, he was being held at a maximum-security federal facility at an undisclosed location. We'd flown there from Arizona the previous night and stayed at a hotel near the airport because there were no accommodations closer to the facility.

The sun was just coming up over the mountains when I roused the kids, got them ready, and hurried them into the car. Visiting hours started promptly at eight A.M., and I knew my father would be waiting. I was excited to see him but also worried about the kids. They didn't see anything different about going to visit their grandfather in a penitentiary. They'd been to prisons before. My brother, Gerard, was in prison and so was my daughter's father, so they were used to visiting people in jail and spending a day. But this visit would be different.

The facility where my father was being held now was also a maximum-security prison with extremely stringent rules about contact with the outside world. The rules said that once Nicholas, Karina, my mother, and I entered, we had to stay inside for a full eight hours. A guard would sit within twenty feet of our table to monitor our conversations. And there wouldn't be much for the kids to do. At the other prisons, they knew there would be TV, card games, and lots of other kids to hang out with. Visiting areas were typically large and could have up to forty inmates receiving visitors at the same time. We'd been told there'd be just one other inmate getting a visit that weekend.

The mood in the car was light. My mother was in the passenger seat, and the kids were playing cards in the back. It was a warm summer day, and for much of the ride I was enjoying the scenery out the driver's side window. One of the things I missed since living in southern Arizona was the greenery and the foliage. When I was a kid growing up in New York, I used to love to play hide-and-seek among the trees in our backyard in Staten Island. It had been almost ten years since I'd left the East Coast, and still I missed it.

We'd been driving for nearly an hour when the piñon pines began to thin, and so did the road, which changed from four lanes to two and from asphalt to dirt. The rocky mixture beneath my tires aggravated my already nervous stomach. I could sense that my daughter's temperament was changing. As the car got closer to the first of the fences surrounding the facility, she suddenly grew quiet and seemed to tense up.

"Mom, is this a bad place for really bad people?" she asked, looking nervously out at the cement watchtowers manned by heavily armed guards. "Worse than the place where my dad and Uncle Gerard are? Because there's a man with a gun up there."

"Why is Papa Bull in a bigger prison than my father?" Nicholas questioned. "Why is it a bigger deal to visit him?"

"Your grandfather is considered a higher profile and more dangerous criminal because he was a gangster, and he was famous," I told them.

The kids fell silent and my mother didn't say a word.

The uniformed guard in the booth directed me to a parking area and told me to wait in the car until somebody came to get us. That's when I started to get real excited. I hadn't seen my father in a long time. I held such good memories of him from my childhood. He'd been such an important person in shaping me and who I am. We'd had our differences over the years, but at thirty-seven, I'd finally arrived at a place where I could move past the anger and accept and love him for who he was. I wanted the kids to know him and I wanted my dad to see how they'd grown up.

We waited only a few minutes before one of the prison guards came out to the car to take us inside. We filled out some paperwork and had to go through a metal detector and be searched for contraband.

"Your father's really excited about the visit," one of the guards told me. "You know your father's a good guy."

"He's crazy," I said, smiling.

"Oh, he's definitely crazy, but he's a good guy."

I glanced toward the kids and noticed that they seemed to lighten up a bit after hearing what the guard had to say about their grandfather. Squinting against the bright sunlight outside, I hurried them out of the visitor center and through a second gate that led deeper into the prison facility. All the buildings were low-slung and looked like army barracks. There were no windows on any of the structures.

The building we entered was smaller than the rest. It had drab cement-block walls and looked like the inside of a cell.

I could see my father standing at the end of the hallway with a guard at his side. He was dressed in the standard prison garb, brown pants, a black belt, black shoes, and a tan long-sleeve button-down shirt. He almost looked like he was in the army, but in a tan uniform instead of a green one.

Even at a distance, he looked frighteningly sick. Because of his Graves' disease he'd lost all of his body hair. Even his eyelashes had fallen off. He was completely bald. His skin was gray and because of the lengthy confinement, he wound up with vitamin deficiencies from lack of sunlight.

My dad was only sixty-five years old, but he looked eighty. His skin was sallow and his cheeks were sunken. As we got closer, I realized he didn't have any teeth. He'd gotten veneers, a thin layer of enamel put on the fronts of his teeth to make his smile whiter, back in the day when he was running with John Gotti. He was in the process of changing them out when he went to prison. While in prison, his teeth had given him nothing but trouble and he eventually ended up directing the jailhouse dentist to remove most of them. I knew he didn't have them, but I thought he'd be wearing his dentures. He hated the false teeth and used to joke that he felt like he had a piano stuck in his mouth when he had them in.

I felt like crying but I didn't want to freak out the kids, so I ran over and hugged him. "It's good to see you, Daddy," I whispered, as tears fell from my eyes. Stepping back, I saw that both kids were staring at him. I realized they had no idea what to expect. They hadn't seen their grandfather in seven years. And all I had to show them were old family photos. Because Nicholas idolized his grandfather, he'd downloaded an old picture of him from the Internet onto his cell phone. But the gaunt, bald, toothless man now standing before him looked nothing like that photo.

Trying to break the tension, my father joked, "Your grand-father looks like Elmer Fudd."

The kids didn't know who Elmer Fudd was, but I laughed.

Nicholas seemed okay with his grandfather, but Karina looked frightened. Technically, the inmates are only allowed a brief kiss or hug. But the guard kept looking away, and my father snuck in a couple of extra kisses and playfully tugged at my daughter's hair. Soon, he had her smiling.

The guard led us to a small windowless room. There was a television and two vending machines that dispensed snacks and soft drinks because we weren't allowed to bring in any food. "I got you guys something," my father said excitedly. He'd saved all his commissary money to buy the kids chips and sodas from the machines.

My father spent the morning catching up with the kids and the details of their lives. One of the guards found us a game of Uno, and we sat around on plastic chairs talking and playing the game. It felt almost like when I was a kid and we were back at the farm in New Jersey where we had spent our summers. We'd sit around the dining room table eating chips and play-ing checkers and cards. My father is very competitive, and he'd let us stay up late as long as we played cards with him. He was like a different person. It was the one place where he could re-lax and be himself.

At the farm, there was never a sense of mob activity. It was laid-back and fun. He'd laugh and joke. I never felt the stress that I could feel when we were back in Staten Island. There, my father was always busy and rarely had time to play. Some nights, I'd find him sitting alone in the kitchen with all the lights turned off. I wouldn't ask him what was wrong. I would come in and make a joke. As soon I started to talk, he'd act normal, like nothing was bothering him. But I could always tell. He'd get real quiet and stare off distractedly.

Knowing now what he was going through, I can almost go back in my mind and pinpoint certain events, like the time his best friend Joe "Stymie" D'Angelo was shot dead in a bar/restaurant that Stymie and my father had bought together. That night, I found him in the kitchen, thinking.

"Do you miss Stymie?" I asked.

"I will always miss Stymie," he said, choking up. It was the only time I ever saw him this upset.

My father is a very dangerous man. He has the ability to kill someone at the drop of a dime. He doesn't belittle people. But if he feels he is being taken advantage of or someone is backing him into a corner, watch out. I didn't know it then, but he was up plotting a murder that night. He was thirsty for revenge and trying to figure out how he was going to execute Stymie's killer, a member of the Colombo crime family who had harassed the female bartender at the restaurant. Looking back, I can recall a number of nights finding my father in the kitchen after midnight.

Thank you guys for being so good," I told the kids during the ride back to the hotel that night. Before dinner, we all went for a swim in the pool. "How do you guys feel about the visit?" I asked, as they splashed around in the deep end.

"Aunt Karen, can I ask you a question?" Nicholas said. "Did Grandpa ever kill anyone?"

Oh my God. We still had another day to go, and I didn't want the kids to be scared of their grandfather. But I didn't want to lie to them.

"Yes, he did," I said matter-of-factly. "It's part of being in the Mafia."

Nicholas persisted. "What's the Mafia?"

I tried to explain as best I could. "What I knew as a kid growing up was that it was a group of Italian men who came to America. It was hard for them to get jobs and stuff, so they came together and formed a secret organization to take care of each other, like a family did. It may have involved stealing and robbing."

"Why did they kill people, then?"

I didn't know how to respond. "Why don't you ask Papa Bull when we see him tomorrow?"

"I don't want him to be mad at me."

That night, I thought about Nicholas and his questions. He reminded me of myself at his age. He was intrigued for different reasons than my daughter. He was trying to make the connections, as I once had.

"Well, what did the kids say?" my father whispered when I hugged him hello the following morning.

"They had a good visit," I smiled.

Glancing over at my nephew, my father said, "So you think your papa's crazy?"

"No, you're good," Nicholas said, shaking my father's hand.

"Dad, Nick has some questions he wants to ask you."

Nicholas crossed his arms in front of him. "No," he murmured.

"What? What is it, Nick?"

"Nothing."

"Dad, he wants to know what a gangster is. And about the

Mafia." I watched my father's face for a reaction but saw none. Taking my nephew by the arm, he led him to one of the plastic chairs along the wall.

"Nick," my father began. "There are certain things that I might not answer, but I'm going to try and guide you."

I couldn't believe it. That's just what he'd said to me some twenty-seven years earlier in the kitchen of our Staten Island home. My father laid out what the Mafia was all about, in terms expressly chosen for his grandchildren. "The Mafia started back in Italy. It was a group of men that got together and formed a brotherhood. They protected their villages and their families. These men built their new brotherhood on trust and loyalty. They would do what was needed to take care of one another and their families. They called this brotherhood Cosa Nostra, Italian for 'our thing.'

"When the Italians started to come to America, a lot of the old-time men worked hard, but they were immigrants and it was hard for them to get jobs, so they started to steal and rob and do whatever they needed to take care of their families.

"As these men started to make money, they earned respect and a lot of the younger men wanted to be a part of the organization, which was now called the Mafia. I wanted to be a part of it, Nick," my father explained.

"I looked up to this brotherhood so much that I wanted to be just like them, even if it meant not always doing the right thing. I liked that it had rules, structure, and organization. To me, it was like being in the army and Cosa Nostra became my government."

My daughter didn't say a word, she just listened.

"Did you ever murder someone?" Nicholas asked in a soft voice.

"I did, but God don't like that, Nick. That's why I'm in here. Looking back now, I realize I took the easy road. Everything that I ever did in life was because I wanted to give my family a better life. And because I made mistakes, I wound up here in prison. I live with what I did every day of my life. So make it all worth it for me. Make sure you never wind up here."

Before we left the prison that day, my father pulled Nicholas aside. "You have to promise Papa Bull one thing. You'll always be a good boy and you'll take care of your aunt, your cousin Karina, and your grandma. Make sure that you go to school. That's important. If something looks too easy, don't take that route."

PART I

CHAPTER ONE

"If we have to go to war, that's what we have to do."

I was nine years old when I began to suspect that my father was a gangster. It was Sunday and Dad had us all packed into the car for an afternoon of house hunting. He loved driving around different neighborhoods, pointing out houses he liked and sharing his renovation ideas. On this particular Sunday, we were cruising around Todt Hill, an upscale community on the southern end of Staten Island, filled with homes owned by doctors, lawyers, and "businessmen."

Mom was in the front seat with Dad, and my younger brother, Gerard, and I were buckled in the back. My father had just finished the renovations on a three-bedroom house he'd bought for us in Bulls Head, a predominantly blue-collar neighborhood just over the Verrazano-Narrows Bridge and not far from the two-bedroom apartment we had been renting in Benson-hurst, Brooklyn.

My father was obsessed with construction and remodeling. He'd ripped apart and remodeled every place we'd ever lived in. He'd started tearing apart the new house the minute we had taken ownership, knocking down walls and putting in improvements, like nice European tiles.

My brother and I attended the local public school, P.S. 60. My mother would walk me to school every day. I had some good friends there, but Dad's friend Louie Milito was forever suggesting that he transfer me to the private prep school on "The Hill." His own daughter, Dina, went there. And so did Dori LaForte. Dori's grandfather was a big player in the Gambino crime family. "The Hill" had large manicured homes dotting its steep streets and was about ten minutes from our three-bedroom house on Leggett Place. Anybody who was anybody lived on "The Hill."

One particular house in this fancy neighborhood belonged to Gambino family crime boss Paul Castellano. We were on one of our Sunday expeditions when Dad pointed it out to us. It was an enormous monster of a house, unlike any other in the neighborhood. It was way fancier and more ornate. It looked more like an Italian villa or a museum, with its iron gates and a gigantic fountain spewing water in the middle of a large, circular brick driveway filled with expensive cars and incredibly manicured grounds. It must have cost a fortune. There was an elaborate security system with surveillance cameras monitoring the perimeter, which seemed to span an entire block.

"Wow," I said. "What does Paul do that he has such a big house?"

"He's in the construction business," my father replied.

I remembered thinking how glad I was that my father worked in the same business as Paul, so that maybe one day we could get a mansion like that. Dad didn't say Paul was his boss in one of New York's biggest, most blood-letting, most feared crime families, or that the construction business wasn't building somebody a little house, but more like construction racketeering, loan-sharking, and extortion. He didn't mention being a businessman like Paul was putting your life on the line. I'd have to wait to learn this angle of the business.

By the fall, my father announced that I was going to be transferring to a new school. He wanted me to get a superior education and had me enrolled at the prestigious Staten Island Academy. I was furious about leaving my friends and worried that I wouldn't fit in with the kids at private school. I was there just a few weeks when a classmate invited me over to her house to play. She lived so close to school, we could see the playground from her yard. It was a beautiful day, and we were outside on her front lawn. Her mother had just gone inside to make us some lemonade when my new friend made a startling announcement.

"My mother and father say a big gangster lives in that house," she said, pointing across the street to the Castellano estate.

I knew that Paul was Dad's friend. I put two and two together and decided if Paul Castellano was a gangster, my father must be one, too. He just didn't act like a gangster. My idea of a gangster was Vito Corleone, the fictional mob boss in *The Godfather*. The movie had even been filmed a few blocks from my school.

Still, I'd been confronted with the possibility that my father was "connected" before. When I was six, I found a gun in my parents' bedroom in our apartment on Sixty-first Street in

Bensonhurst. Mom was in the kitchen, and I was amusing myself by hiding some of my favorite books under their bed. That's when I came upon the pistol Dad had stuffed beneath the mattress. I knew my father had served in the army during the Vietnam War because I'd seen his dog tags. I wondered if this was a souvenir from the war. Racing to the kitchen, I went to ask my mother about my startling discovery.

"Mommy, does Daddy have a gun because he was in the army?"

"Yeah" was all she could muster.

The next day, I bragged to my friends at school, telling them my father had a gun under the bed because he was in the army. My teacher overheard me and went directly to my mother. When Dad found out, he wasn't upset. He just told me not to talk about it anymore.

My father had this "coolness" about him. He was hipper than the other kids' dads. He wore sweats and gold chains, and he had tattoos, Jesus on one arm and a rose on the other. He also had a small diamond in the middle of his chest. He owned nightclubs and always stayed out late. Some of his friends were bouncers. They spoke and dressed differently from the dads of the other kids at school. They had wads of cash in their pockets and always came bearing gifts, even if it was just a box of pastries on Sunday.

On weekends, my father would sometimes take me with him to "the club" in Bensonhurst. I didn't know it then, but it was a local mobster hangout, also known as a men's "social club." Dad would first get the car washed and then we'd stop in. Guys would be playing cards and drinking coffee. The club looked like a big kitchen, with tables and chairs set out around the room and a few pictures, mostly scenes of Italy, hanging on the walls. There were no women around, ever. An older man named "Toddo" was usually at one of the tables in the back. He was always nicely dressed in slacks and a sweater, sporting a big, fancy watch and a pinky ring.

"Hey Bo, what's up?" my father would say. It's how he addressed everyone, even me. I didn't know why he addressed people as Bo, not Bro.

"Go say hello to Uncle Toddo," he'd instruct, pushing me in the old man's direction.

I'd have to go over and hug and kiss him. "How you doing, kiddo?" he'd ask. The old man would pat me on the head and then stick a twenty-dollar bill in my pocket.

I thought it was weird the way the men all kissed each other on one cheek and then exchanged a firm handshake. No one just walked into a room and said hello; it was always a handshake, and there always seemed to be an order of whose hand should be shaken first. Obviously, I didn't know that Toddo was Salvatore "Toddo" Aurello, a capo in the Gambino crime family, and my father's boss and mentor in the mob. I just thought Dad respected him more because he was older.

It wasn't until I was twelve years old that I knew for certain that my father was a gangster. Even then, I knew not to ask any questions.

When I was in middle school, I overheard my parents talking about some guy who wanted to buy one of my father's nightclubs. It was late afternoon and we were all over at my aunt Fran's for Sunday dinner. Fran was one of my father's older sisters. She and her husband, Eddie, lived across the street from us in a two-family house. Dad's mother also lived there, in an apartment downstairs.

Aunt Fran was closer to my father than his sister Jean. Dad and Fran were closer in age and seemed to have more in common. Fran was always warm and loving. She played the piano, and she taught Gerard and me how to play. She'd sit us down and tell us stories about my grandparents, and how they had come over from Italy. My father's mother, Kay, wrote children's stories that were published here in the United States. Aunt Fran would read us those stories, and she'd add to them with her own fanciful fabrications. One of Grandma Kay's stories was about a little girl named Karen and a rabbit. Another one was about my cousins and how they flew through the city on the wings of an eagle. My Aunt Jean, or Jeannie, who was Dad's eldest sister, kept the books at her house, but they were all lost in a fire after Grandma Gravano died. Jeannie was married to my uncle Angelo. He wasn't involved in "the life." He was an engineer.

Jeannie was much older than Dad. We would go over to their house a lot. Uncle Angelo was into golf and tennis, and he had a fish tank in his basement. We weren't allowed to touch any of his things. Dad loved Angelo. He was more like a father figure to Sammy. Uncle Angelo was a hard man, but he was very generous. He had a lot of morals, and he stood behind his morals. When two of his kids got in trouble for smoking marijuana, he threw them out of the house. Dad couldn't relate to that type of discipline; no matter what I did, he would never disown me.

On the nights that Dad worked late in Brooklyn, we'd usually go over to Aunt Fran's for dinner. Dad would meet us there when he got home. He had this thing about eating together as a family every night, and made it a point to be home at five sharp.

I remember sitting around the long white table in Aunt Fran's dining room when Dad started telling everybody about this Czechoslovakian guy named Frank Fiala. He said the guy was "nuts." I wasn't sure what this guy was doing that made Dad think he was out of his mind, but whatever it was, it was beginning to piss off my father. I knew that Frank Fiala wanted to buy The Plaza Suite on Sixty-eighth Street in Gravesend, Brooklyn. It was my father's most successful nightclub. Dad owned the entire building and operated The Plaza Suite out of the second floor. His construction company headquarters and a showroom for his carpet and wood flooring company were on the ground floor. The discotheque was enormous. It spanned the entire five thousand square feet of the building and had a bar, a dance floor, and a private VIP lounge. People lined up outside for hours hoping to get in. For a time, Dad was there practically every night, but with his construction business demanding more of his time, he was looking to unload the place.

Frank offered my father a million dollars for the club. Dad had accepted his offer, but I think he was starting to have second thoughts. A few days after we first heard about Frank Fiala, my father didn't show up for dinner. I'd been waiting for him to get home so I could ask him if my best friend, Toniann, could sleep over. Mom said I needed Dad's permission. He almost always said yes.

Six o'clock rolled around and he still wasn't home.

"Where's Daddy?" I asked my mother.

She looked up from her pot of tomato sauce. "Your father is busy. He won't be joining us for dinner."

"Well, can Toniann sleep over?"

"Let's wait until your father gets home and see what he says."

"But you just said he's not coming home for dinner. When will he be back?"

"I don't know. And honestly, I don't know if this is a good night for Toniann to be here anyhow. Maybe she should go home now." She packed up the sauce in plastic containers. "We're going across the street to eat with your grandmother, Aunt Fran, and the kids. Get your brother, put on some clean clothes, and let's get going."

There was a strange vibe in Aunt Fran's house that evening. Uncle Eddie wasn't around, which was also odd. None of the adults said anything while they set out the food, a sure sign something was wrong because my family members were big talkers. Even though I wanted to, I didn't ask Mom any more questions.

After dinner, I asked her if I could go across the street to Toniann's to play until my father came home. "You can play, but only for half an hour."

"What about the sleepover?" I pressed.

She sighed. "Ask your father when he gets home. If he doesn't come home, it'll have to be another night."

We were out playing in Toniann's front yard when Uncle Eddie's car roared around the corner and screeched into our driveway. Dad jumped out and ran into our house, and I ran in after him. He wasn't in the living room or the kitchen, so I wandered upstairs. The door to the bedroom was shut. The moment I cracked it opened, Dad turned and looked at me with a serious face.

"Don't you knock?" He quickly turned his back to me, but not before I saw him jam a revolver into the waistband of his jeans. I tried to figure out if something was wrong, but his body language revealed nothing. He was calm and together. I stared at him and struggled to convince myself that I hadn't seen the gun. After a long pause, I finally said, "I was just going to ask if I could have a sleepover with . . ."

He interrupted, "No, you can't!" He untucked his T-shirt and turned around to face me.

"Why not?" I whined. "What's the big deal?"

"Not tonight. You can have one over the weekend. And I can't talk about this right now. I gotta go." His eyes were cold; I felt as if he was looking through me. He spoke really quickly, his mind clearly somewhere else. He grabbed a pair of black leather gloves off the top of his dresser and brushed by me.

I followed him into the hallway, watched him stomp down the stairs, and called after him, "Why do you need the gloves? It's the middle of the summer." I knew in my heart that something bad was about to happen, and I was terrified.

He stopped, stared, and said, "Why do you ask so many questions?"

"I don't know. I was just asking."

"One day, you're gonna make a good lawyer." He slowly came back up the stairs, bent down, and kissed me on the forehead. "I promise you can have a sleepover before we leave for the farm next week." The farm was Dad's pride and joy, a thirty-acre working horse farm he'd purchased and renovated in rural New Jersey. We'd spent every summer there since Dad bought the place.

"Trust me, tonight's not a good night," my father told me. "Now I want you to be a good girl. You're the oldest. You're in charge and you have to take care of your brother. And don't drive your mother nuts." He kissed me again, stood up, and headed out the door.

My father had an uncanny ability to make me feel that everything was okay no matter what the circumstances. Even seeing him leave the house with a gun tucked in his pants that night seemed fine.

My mother was in the kitchen and missed the whole conversation. I didn't bother to tell her what I'd seen.

The following morning, the headline in the newspaper on our kitchen table said: MURDER OUTSIDE THE PLAZA SUITE. Dad was in the kitchen acting normal. I didn't even know if he saw me reading the article. I didn't have time to read it all, but I noticed that the victim was Frank Fiala.

I knew the guy had been doing some things to annoy my father. But murder? I stopped reading the minute my father sat down at the breakfast table. Neither of us said a word.

Later that week, Dad ordered my mother to pack up my brother and me and head to the farm in Cream Ridge. When Dad had bought the place, it was pretty dilapidated. But he said it had potential and a lot of property. My father fell in love with it immediately. As soon as we took ownership, he was knocking down walls and doing his elaborate renovations. Soon, the run-down old farmhouse with a couple of barns and some rusty farm equipment became a spectacular estate with an in-ground pool. It had a state-of-the-art facility for training and boarding horses and a professional racetrack in the front yard. The track was an exact replica of the Freehold Raceway in New Jersey. My father hired a trainer from the barn in Staten Island where my brother and I took lessons and built a small house for him on the property. Most of the horses the trainer worked with were trotters that competed at Meadowlands Racetrack. My father even restored the old horse-drawn carriage that was left behind by a previous owner.

It bothered me that we were leaving for the farm so suddenly and without Dad. We weren't even supposed to be going for another few days. The farm was a place where my family would always have fun. There was always something to do there. It was about an hour and forty-five minutes south of Staten Island in the historic town of Cream Ridge. The area was so rural compared to Staten Island. It had hills covered in trees, narrow two-lane roads, and lots of large horse farms. It took five minutes just to get down the bumpy dirt road that dead-ended in our driveway.

The main house was enormous and had breathtaking views of our thirty acres of grassy land. The exterior had been white when we bought it, but was now gray. It was surrounded by a beautiful stone porch that had a big table and lots of outdoor chairs. I adored that house. My bedroom was upstairs with a view of the track, which I loved. I was into horseback riding and spent hours with Snowflake, my beautiful white pony. In Staten Island, I rode on an English saddle, but it was Western at the farm.

We spent most of the summer in Cream Ridge. Mom liked to putter around in the garden and my brother, Gerard, kept himself busy dirt biking around the vast property. During the summer, Dad commuted back and forth. He'd leave the farm on a Tuesday and come back on Thursday. My father was a different person when he was at the farm. He'd sit out on the front porch in the mornings, sipping coffee and watching the trainers on the track. He always seemed relaxed, as though he didn't have a care in the world.

He'd bring friends and their families from New York. I didn't know it at the time, but all the friends were involved in the Mafia. My father had one rule. There was to be no shoptalk at the farm. "If you come up, you need to bring your coveralls because everyone is pitching in," he'd say. We shared lots of laughs. There were always people around and construction going on.

But the day Dad sent us to the farm early, things didn't go according to the rule. First, he arrived unexpectedly. It was just before dinner when I heard the crunch of gravel on the driveway. Sprinting to the window, I saw Dad's maroon Lincoln pulling up, and several other cars arriving behind his. My father had told us he wouldn't be coming for several more days. And yet here he was. Not only that, he had "Stymie" with him in the car. Stymie was Joe D'Angelo, my father's closest friend.

Dad said he had met him on the "street." The two men were so simpatico they even looked alike with their dark brown hair and short stocky builds, although at five feet eight inches tall Stymie had a good three inches on my father. They dressed the same, too, in similar sweat suits and sneakers. Stymie owned a bar in Brooklyn called Docks. Dad referred to him as his right-hand man.

My father was in his white T-shirt and sweatpants when he stepped out of the car. Stymie was wearing a sweatshirt over his shirt. He didn't have his wife with him, which was very unusual. When Dad's friends came up, they always brought their families. Uncle Eddie and several other members of Dad's work crew got out of the other vehicles. None of them had their wives and kids along.

I ran around to the kitchen to say hello to my father. He was talking to my mother in a hushed voice. I saw her shaking her head.

"Okay," she whispered, before following my dad outside.

That night, Mom served dinner out on the back porch, which was completely screened in. There was a low wall around the base of the porch supporting the screens. When I wanted to eavesdrop on my parents' conversations I could hide behind it, out of view. I'd often use the spot to overhear discussions about requests of mine, like when I would ask my parents if we could go to Great Adventure Amusement Park. After I had asked, I'd disappear from the room and then sneak around back and listen from the outside to hear them weighing their decision.

That evening, however, I sensed my father was not himself. His mood was scaring me. I could always tell when something was on his mind. He'd get quiet and stare off into space. I was sure something was wrong and was convinced it had to do with the gun and the murder outside his nightclub. I didn't want to think that he might be involved.

"Go help your mom clean up," my father told me at the end of dinner. I cleared the table, and then asked my father if he wanted to watch me ride Snowflake.

"No, I'll come out later," he said. "I'm just talking to the boys."

Mom was in the kitchen when I snuck around to the outside of the porch and crawled into my hiding spot. My back was against the wall and I was sitting, "Indian-style," listening. I'd never done that before, listening in on one of my father's conversations with his friends. But I wanted to know what was going on.

"Paul's hot over this," I heard one of the guy's say. I knew they were probably talking about Paul Castellano. He was Dad's boss in the construction business, or so I thought.

"Well I had to do what I had to do," I heard my father say. "Fuck Paul. If we have to go to war, that's what we have to do."

War? What was my father talking about?

I heard Uncle Eddie interrupt. "I told you we shouldn't have done this."

"All right, Eddie, stop with your whining," Dad snapped.

Something was definitely wrong. My father could be in trouble. I was sure it had to do with what had happened the night I'd seen him with the revolver. I was starting to put the pieces together. After I had seen him with the gun, I found out that the guy who was buying his nightclub had been murdered, and now my father was saying that he "did what he had to do." I started thinking of all the things I'd seen and heard over the years that hadn't made sense, like the time when I was six and found the gun under his mattress and him being out late and hanging out with people who looked different from my friends' fathers. I wanted to stay and listen some more, but I was worried about being seen. I was also feeling guilty about hearing stuff that was clearly not meant for me to hear. I crawled away and went back into the house through the front door.

At that moment, my father walked back into the kitchen.

"I thought you were going riding," he said.

"I'm not in the mood." I could feel my father staring at me like he knew I had been listening.

"Are you okay?" He was looking at me weird.

"Yeah, why?"

"Let's cut up some fruit and we'll bring it out to the guys," he smiled.

I watched him at the kitchen counter, carefully slicing the

skin from the watermelon. Following him out to the porch, I continued to study him, observing how he was interacting with the guys. My father was at ease, talking and enjoying his dessert. He seemed back to his normal self. I was confused. Maybe I was just misreading him.

Later that evening, Dad and I walked out to the barn to turn out the lights. Snowflake was kicking at her stall, happy to see us. "You guys are going to go back to Staten Island for a couple of days," he said.

"Why, I thought we were going to stay up here for the whole summer?"

"You are," he smiled. "But you're just gonna go back to Staten Island for a couple of days."

I was back to thinking that something wasn't right. What I'd just overheard, the gun, the man who just got shot outside Dad's nightclub.

"Daddy, if you ever die, would we live up here on the farm?" I was beginning to feel a little frightened.

My father stood still. Turning to look at me, he asked, "Why would you ask that?"

"I don't know. I just want to know if we'd live in Staten Island or come up to the farm to live."

"Well, I don't think you're going to have to worry about that 'cause you're stuck with me for a long time."

I didn't know there was a hit out on his life.

The next morning, Gerard and I came downstairs. We went out to the chicken coop to look for eggs for our breakfast. The hens laid brown eggs, which had taken me a while to get used to, but I grew to love them. We found two eggs, but broke one in the fight over who was carrying them. Mom said we'd have to use one from the refrigerator, but she wasn't going to tell us who was getting which. Gerard and I loved our eggs sunny-side up, which we called "dunky" eggs because of the nice puddle of yolk to dunk our toast in.

By the time we got the egg issue straightened out, Dad was at the breakfast table acting normal. I was looking at him, not sure what to think. The night before something was definitely wrong, but he always just made everything seem like it was okay. I was too scared to ask any questions. My mom seemed a little preoccupied. When we left for Staten Island, she told my father, "I love you," then hugged him in a way that was different. Because he was so calm, I wasn't as nervous as I might have been otherwise. We went to the barn to feed my horse and say good-bye. I found Dad still in the kitchen and kissed him goodbye. "I'll see you guys soon," he said. Mom had a big, white percolator pot going on the stove, and Dad's friends were outside on the back porch drinking coffee.

When we got back to Staten Island, a bunch of our friends were playing outside. Gerard and I jumped out of the car to join them, forgetting all about the disturbing situation back at the farm. I was so excited to see my friends. It was like nothing ever happened. Dad came back from Cream Ridge a couple of days later. I was so happy to see him, and I hugged him for an extra long time. I looked at him like nothing could ever happen to us, not with him to protect us. He seemed like his normal self again. He even called Gerard and me "kiddo." After dinner, he told me that I needed to rub his head. One of our favorite routines when I wanted to stay up late was to rub his head, face, and shoulders. Normally, he pretended he had to bribe me to rub his head, pay me. But this time I did it willingly, I was just so happy to see him. I was just so relieved.

I didn't think about Frank Fiala at all. I was too young to grasp that murder was part of Dad's job description. I didn't even know that Fiala's murder was against the rules of the Mafia because it hadn't been authorized by the boss, Paul Castellano. In that world, before you could commit murder, you had to make a case to the family capo. An unsanctioned murder usually cost you your life. Dad was in deep shit, but I didn't know it. There was so much more I had yet to learn.

CHAPTER TWO

"They are bad people, but they are our bad people."

My father was a gangster even before I was born. My parents lived in Bensonhurst when I made my appearance in the maternity ward of St. John's Catholic Hospital on Fourth Avenue in Brooklyn on May 8, 1972. My parents, Debra Scibetta and Salvatore "Sammy" Gravano, couldn't have been more proud. My mother was eighteen and my father was twenty-six. They were still newlyweds, married for just over a year.

My mother's twin sister, Diane, had introduced the two. Diane knew my father from the neighborhood. In Bensonhurst, Brooklyn's Little Italy, everybody knew everybody. There were blocks and blocks of identical, detached two-story houses with little fenced yards and street parking. In the pizzerias and bakeries along Eighteenth Avenue, everybody spoke Italian and knew the names of all the babies in the carriages. Sundays were for church, big meals, and family.

My aunt Diane was more outspoken than my mother and hung out with more people in the neighborhood. My mother was reserved and very shy and didn't go out that often. She was a pretty brunette. She had a great figure and a radiance of innocence, and my father was smitten. She wasn't into clothing and fashion, although she always looked nice in an understated way. What he liked about her best was that she was not like the girls who frequented his after-hours club in Fort Hamilton, who wore lots of makeup and acted slutty. My father was instantly attracted to my mother. He said he knew she was the one for him. He could tell right away that she would be a devoted wife and mother. They dated for less than a year before they were married.

When my father first asked my grandparents, Sandra and John Scibetta, for my mother's hand, they were not too thrilled. Sammy had a reputation as a thug. He'd had a couple of run-ins with the law and had been in lots of fights. My mother's parents knew my father's parents, aunts, and uncles and knew them to be good people. Still, at the time Sammy was a member of the Rampers, a prominent Brooklyn street gang. The Rampers were involved in armed robberies, burglaries, car thefts, and extortion, rising hoods heading for a life of crime. They'd started off with "trunking," robbing people's trunks for spare tires. Unbeknownst to his future in-laws, my father was also a recently inducted "associate" of the Colombo crime family under Joseph Colombo.

But Sammy had been very respectful and charming with their daughter, so they begrudgingly gave him their blessing, saying they would have to wait until Debra turned eighteen.

They didn't think Sammy would be able to marry their daughter anytime soon, anyway, because catering halls for the reception were booked a year in advance. They were certain the romance would fizzle out by then.

Sammy had a connection at the Colonial Mansion, a splashy catering hall on Bath Avenue and Twenty-second Street with marble floors and crystal chandeliers and was able to get the hall in less than one month. The wedding itself took place at St. Bernadette's Church on Friday, April 16, 1971, one month shy of Debbie's eighteenth birthday. More than three hundred people, mostly from the neighborhood and including a few wiseguys, were there to witness the union and join in the celebration afterward at the Colonial Mansion.

Everybody was hoping that once Sammy settled down and had children, he would abandon his criminal ways. They weren't too far off the mark, because after I was born, our family moved out of Brooklyn to my father's parents' house in Ronkonkoma, a town on Long Island, about an hour east of Bensonhurst. My father had spent his childhood summers in the tiny house that eventually became my grandparents' permanent home. When our family moved out there, my grandparents happily converted the attic into living quarters for us. My father was determined to go straight and to find honest work. His epiphany came at a moment of desperation, when he and my mother had to bust open my piggy bank to be able to buy enough food for dinner.

His brother-in-law, Eddie Garafola, his sister Fran's husband, offered him work. Eddie was a partner in a small construction business in Ronkonkoma that specialized in plumbing, and had plenty for him to do. My father started working long hours, but was still earning less than one hundred dollars a week. When he asked Eddie for a raise, my uncle and his partner told him that ten cents more an hour was all they could spare. Peeved, Sammy went to work for another construction company that was run by a friend of my mother's uncle. There, he started at $175 a week, but within ten months, was making $250. He was beginning to feel optimistic about being able to provide for his family legitimately in the construction business.

The family was out on Long Island for less than one year when my father and another guy, Alley Boy Cuomo, were indicted for the murders of two brothers, Arthur and Joseph Dunn from Coney Island. The two had operated a local auto body shop, but had not made good on a loan when they were gunned down in 1969. Based on information from a thug already in jail on something else, my father and Alley Boy were arrested. The thug wanted to get his sentence shortened and offered up my father and Alley Boy for shaking him down a couple of years earlier. My father knew he was being framed, he had never heard of the Dunn brothers. But that didn't help with his arrest.

My father's boss in the Gambino family, Toddo Aurello, loaned him ten thousand dollars to make bail, on the condition that he pay him back, with interest. Because he also needed money to pay his legal bills and support the family, we had to go back to Bensonhurst. We moved into my mom's parents' five-room apartment on Fifteenth Avenue. My aunt Diane was still living at home and we all shared her small bedroom, while she slept on a couch in the living room.

Back in the same old neighborhood, my father was doing the same bad things every night, robbing and stealing to get enough money to pay for the lawyers for his defense. He said he didn't do the murders, it was a made-up case, but he still had to mount a defense. He didn't have any other way to make the kind of money he needed to pay the legal fees. To make matters worse, he was arrested three times while he was out on bail, so his legal bills were mounting.

Two weeks before the double murder case was scheduled to go to trial, it was dismissed because there were so many inconsistencies in the guy's story. In one of them, the thug had claimed my father was driving a white '72 Lincoln, but Sammy didn't own that car until years after the murders. Even though my dad was cleared, there was no turning back from his life of crime. His attorney's fees had left him in debt. He realized that if he was going to be in the business of crime, he was going to do it one hundred percent. That was my father's motto, whatever he did, he did it one hundred percent, whether he was a criminal, a father, or someone cooperating with the authorities, whatever choices he made, he was going to follow through with no turning back.

Soon, he started pulling in enough money to rent his own apartment and moved us out of my grandparents' home and into an apartment on Sixty-first Street.

My mother was one of those very loyal wives who would stand by her man through thick and thin and ask no questions. She never really questioned my father because she believed in her heart that he meant well. I know she wished they had never left Long Island and her dream for a simple life. As the mother of his children, she supported whatever decisions he made. I'm sure at times she wished that it could have been different, but she understood that when the breadwinners came home from a long day, they didn't tell the wives what they did, and the women didn't ask questions. So, she surrounded herself with her kids, her sister, her parents, and some of the wives of the men in my father's crew who understood this lifestyle.

Neither of my sets of grandparents was involved in the mob. My maternal grandmother and grandfather both worked to provide for their family. My grandfather worked nights for the Western Electric Telephone Company, putting together circuit boards, and my grandmother had a job at a dry cleaners. They had been able to save enough money to buy a summer home in Pennsylvania, where they could escape from the city.

My father's parents came to America from Italy. The family was very poor. All the men in the family had come first, then sent for the women and children. My grandfather, "Giorlando" in Italy but "Gerry" here, was the youngest boy and was the last to come. He was in his mid-teens when he traveled alone by freighter from Sicily to Canada. When the boat reached Canada, he jumped ship, and he had to find his way to New York with only a telephone number. Because he slipped into the United States illegally, he was never able to get his U.S. citizenship. He was very Italian, abided by his strict Italian traditions, and spoke either Italian or very broken English in a strong Italian accent.

My father's mother was Caterina, but everyone called her Kay. She had been born in the United States, and raised her three children to speak English, knowing they would need it to be successful here. As a kid, I remember thinking how strange it was that my grandmother, aunts, and father spoke English well, but my grandfather did not.

When Grandpa Gravano first got to New York, he found work as a house painter. I don't know how he met my grandmother, but she was a seamstress when they got married. Grandpa's exposure to so much paint gave him lead poisoning, so my grandmother, always an ambitious and hardworking woman, supported them. My grandmother's boss helped her open a dress factory in Bensonhurst, and my grandfather helped her run it. I remember my grandmother always wearing nice dresses. She walked a lot, which helped her keep her nice shape.

My grandparents had their children later in life, delayed by a couple of miscarriages. Finally, they produced three children, first two daughters, Jeannie and Fran, and then a son, Salvatore. Dad's parents called him "Sammy" because he had such a resemblance to his uncle Sammy. The name stuck. He was my grandmother's "baby."

Even though my grandparents were not involved with the Mafia, a lot of Mafia members lived in their neighborhood. In Sicily, where Cosa Nostra started, the members protected their neighborhoods. When they came over from Italy, they also felt like they were protecting their communities and they were very respected. Grandpa Gravano was familiar with the Mafia culture and always treated the members with appropriate respect. They would be hanging around outside of the social clubs when my grandfather and my dad would pass on their way to the dress factory. They knew my grandfather's name and would always shout hello across the street. My father was curious how my grandfather knew them. My grandfather explained that they weren't hardworking, nice people. "They are bad people, but they are our bad people," he would say.

He told my father that they were the ones the Italian community would turn to when they had problems to resolve. There was a lot of anti-Italian sentiment back then, and Italians found it better to take care of business like they did in the Old Country. He made it clear that they should be respected but avoided.

My father said he was the kind of kid who got into fights in the playground at school. He was a lousy student, which caused him to be humiliated and teased mercilessly. The only way he could be respected was to take it outside. There, the bullies would leave him alone. When my dad was in fourth grade, he was held back for a learning disability. He had a severe case of dyslexia, but at the time his teachers assessed him as being mentally retarded. He tried to laugh it off by being the class clown. But using his fists to take down troublemakers was easier and more satisfying, so anyone who dared to tease him was beat up after school.

On Sammy's tenth birthday, my grandparents bought him a new bike. Some kids stole it, but Sammy spotted it one week later across the street from the social club. When he went to claim it, he took on the two kids who refused to give it back. He put up a valiant fight, earning him the nickname "little bull" from a couple of wiseguys who watched the whole thing go down.

When my father was thirteen, he got a taste of the power of the men in the mob. One day, he was at the dress factory helping my grandfather with the payroll.

A couple of Irish-looking thugs came into the office. They said they were from the union and threatened my grandfather, saying he would have to either start making payoffs or unionize the place or face getting his legs busted up. My father was very upset by the disrespect they showed him. His father told him that everything was under control, Zuvito would fix it.

Sammy knew Zuvito was an old, frail guy from the neighborhood. He couldn't fight two brawny, angry Irish thugs. His

Rampers buddies gave him a gun and advised him to blow the two guys away. When Monday morning came around, the men arrived as scheduled. But this time they were completely friendly and apologetic. They said they didn't know Zuvito was Gerry's *compadre,* everything was good, and everybody shook hands.

Sammy was stunned. His father again said there was nothing to worry about. Zuvito was a powerful person, a bad guy but "our bad guy."

When Sammy showed his father the gun, Gerry was livid. He glared at his son, took the gun, and said that the Gravanos were legitimate, honest people. He said if they had problems, they go to people like Zuvito for help. My grandfather didn't hit him, but my father said this was probably the closest he had ever come.

Eventually, Sammy learned the truth that Zuvito and the other guys who hung around in front of the social clubs were gangsters. He decided he wanted the lifestyle. The fights in the playground were escalating. He was a miserable failure academically. At sixteen, his parents were forced to sign him out of school and his formal education was over.

My father preferred life with the Rampers, anyway. Gang life was exciting and reaped big payoffs for the brazen ones. Many Rampers aspired to be in the Mafia, and my father was "a good earner," meaning he had the necessary makings to be a gangster. He was loyal, he was a moneymaker, he was a natural leader, and he had the ability to "whack" somebody.

He soon caught the eye of Joe Colombo, the head of the Colombo crime family. Colombo remembered that my father had beat up his two sons at a movie theater a couple of years earlier. Colombo hadn't held that against him. In fact, he liked the fact that my father had let them go before he totally broke their asses. Colombo made Sammy an "associate" in his organization, along with his Rampers' buddy Tommy Spero. By being associates, both of them answered to "made" members of the Mafia. To become "made," an associate had to be sponsored by a "made" man. At the time, the "books" of the crime families were closed and had been for eleven years. Both men were hopeful that they were going be brought in when the books reopened.

My father was assigned to the crew of Thomas "Shorty" Spero, Tommy's uncle. His first job was to rob a clothing store, and his second assignment was a bank. After both those holdups, he was arrested but managed to escape conviction after witnesses changed their minds about testifying.

My father had been a Colombo family associate for two years when he was asked to whack somebody for the first time. He was just twenty-five years old the day he shot his victim, Joe Colucci, two times in the back of the head with a Beatles' tune playing in the background. The word was that Colucci, a fellow Colombo associate, was going to whack Sammy, so Sammy was authorized by Colombo capo Carmine Persico to take him out first. At four in the morning, after a night of club hopping, Joe, Sammy, Tommy Spero, and another guy, Frankie, got into a car. Sammy was in the backseat, and Joe was in front of him in the passenger seat. Driving down the Belt Parkway in Brooklyn at a pretty good speed, Sammy placed two bullets in Joe's head, told the driver to get off in a residential neighborhood, and dumped Joe facedown in the street. He fired three bullets into his body to be sure the hit was complete.

After that, Sammy found himself with a different kind of respect. He now had clout and prestige in certain circles. He was no longer waiting in line to get into discos and clubs, and the bosses loved him. He was well on his way to becoming a mobster.

Sammy didn't stay long with the Colombo family. Ralph and Shorty Spero were a little jealous about the attention he was getting and worried he would be "made" before Shorty's nephew, young Tommy. With everybody's blessing, my father was transferred to the Gambino family, where he fell under the mentoring of Uncle Toddo. Shortly after, he became a "made" man, someone with full membership in the Cosa Nostra brotherhood. During a secret induction ceremony, conducted in the basement of one of the bosses' homes, he swore his loyalty to the Gambino organization. One of the men asked him which finger he used when he pulled the trigger of a gun, and when he presented his index finger, the man pricked it and smeared some blood on a picture of a saint. Sammy held the picture on his palms while it was set on fire, hearing the admonishment that if he broke his allegiance he would burn in hell just like the depiction of the saint. He also swore to honor *Omertà*, the code of silence. When the ceremony was over, he had all the privileges and protection of a "made" man. But the dues were he had to kill for the Brotherhood, too. He described his induction as being one of the proudest moments of his life, even though the burning of the saint left painful white blisters all over his palms.

CHAPTER THREE

"See? You learn something new every day."

Gerard and I were the other accomplishments dad was proud of. I still remember when Gerard was born. I was three years old, and I was completely grossed out that he was a boy. I wanted a sister, a little doll that I could dress up. I was jealous of him the moment he came home from the hospital. I had been the first and only child, and not only that, I was the very first grandchild on my mother's side. Now Gerard was getting most of the attention. From the moment he was born, he was the apple of my mother's eye. Gerard was her little man. It was probably fair, because the minute I had been born, I had been the apple of my father's eye. Looking back, I can say that I am so much like our father, and Gerard is so much like our mother. Both Mom and Gerard are quiet, nonconfrontational, and kindhearted. Dad and I, on the other hand, are hotheaded, stubborn, loyal, and loving.

My first introduction to my father's not-so-normal life happened around the time Gerard arrived. I was in kindergarten and the kids in our class were asked to sell candy door-to-door to raise money for a class trip. There were incentive prizes for the good salespeople, and I had my eye on the popcorn maker. The machine was one of the bigger prizes, so I knew I had my work cut out for me. Once the teacher handed out our fundraising packets, I wanted to get started right away, making the neighbors commit to buying from me before somebody else in the class got to them. Unfortunately, the weather did not cooperate, and it was raining too hard after school to get out.

My father told me not to worry about it, that he would buy all the candy required for me to earn my popcorn maker. I didn't think that was the way it was supposed to be done. As far as I knew, the rules were that I had to sell the stuff door-to-door, and I didn't want to cheat and get in trouble.

Dad made a deal with me. He said he would take the candy to the after-hours club he owned and sell it to all the guys who worked there. That way, I would still be selling my goods to a lot of different people, even though technically I wouldn't be going to houses in the neighborhood. I liked the plan, and we closed the agreement with a handshake.

The next morning when I woke up, my collection envelope was busting with cash. The sheet where I was supposed to register the names of my buyers was filled with odd names like Sally Dogs and Big Louie, and none of the names was followed by an address, as they were on my classmates's sheets. But there was no question I had sold enough candy to get the popcorn maker. I was looking at stacks of money, hundreds of dollars.

I proudly took the order form and the money to my teacher. She was not impressed with my success. She promptly called my mother to school to discuss the situation. She was sure I had made up the list and taken the money from somebody in the house to win the prize, despite my pleas that the list was honest. I knew my father would never have steered me wrong.

When my mother arrived at school, she assured my teacher that all my customers were real people and that I had worked hard for the cause. I got my popcorn maker, with enough points left over to win a few more things. I settled for just the popcorn maker so I didn't have to feel too greedy. That was the only prize I really wanted, anyway.

I really liked living in Brooklyn. We had so many relatives living nearby, and Gerard and I were always busy and indulged. We'd go to the playground in Gravesend Park for hours and hours to play on the swings or bounce on the big plastic animals on springs. On a good day, we'd get an Italian ice when the Good Humor man came around.

I remember a particular Sunday trip to the duck pond. My father and mother took my older cousins and us to feed the ducks. We each had two slices of stale bread we could rip apart and toss at our leisure. My cousin Mary held on to her crust too long, and a duck bit her finger. My father chased it down the path and caught it before it could escape into the water. What happened next left us all traumatized; the duck was squawking, the kids were screaming, and the feathers were flying as Dad snapped the bird's neck. It was a nightmare. But that was my father's instinct, to protect the people he loved. He felt compelled to protect us, even if he sometimes went well beyond the accepted bounds.

My mother was very nurturing. If I had a question, she always had a way of answering me without answering me. They were never satisfactory answers, and I had to fill in the parts she didn't tell me. I was probably wrong most of the time, but I couldn't keep pestering her.

She was very down to earth and simple. She preferred cooking a meal at home to going out to restaurants. She knew how to make dinner work with very small means and how to improvise.

Even when we were broke, it always seemed like we had plenty of food. She could make a meal out of macaroni and ricotta five different ways by adding peas, or cutting up pieces of chicken. Oven-hot garlic bread was the touch I loved the most.

At our house, we had a family dinner routine. The table was set in a nook, and my dad always sat at the head. I sat to his right, Gerard sat on the bench across from me, and Mom sat at the other end. Every night, Dad had us go around the table sharing something new we had discovered in the last twenty-four hours. When we were done, he would say, "See? You learn something new every day." He was proud that there was always something.

My mother was a woman of very few words. If anything was wrong, especially with my father, she always made sure that my brother and I never learned about it. She shielded us with the same protective instinct as he did, but she just delivered it in a more understated style. She was the kind of mother who would create fake report cards so we didn't get in trouble with my father.

She was so quiet I always assumed she was weak and submissive, but not in a bad way, more like a dutiful way. Not asking questions was not a feeble shortcoming, it was respecting that family members didn't gain anything by prying all the time. I never realized how much strength there was in her silence until I was much older.

My father was the big jokester in the family. He was always playfully teasing my mother, and she was so amiable about being on the receiving end. You could tell that she loved him to death. It didn't seem to bother her that Dad was out all night. If he was out late, I'd always sleep in his spot in the bed until he came home. He would pick me up and move me into my bedroom, whatever hour it was. Mom and he never seemed to have any fights about where he was, and she always appeared to be very understanding about his unconventional work schedule. I wouldn't say they were over-the-top super affectionate. But when Dad came home and lay on the couch, he would put his head on Mom's lap and she would stroke his hair.

Lots of times I wanted to ask my mother questions about what Dad really did for a living, but I knew she wouldn't answer them. She was the family ostrich. She'd just bury her head when things arose that she didn't want to deal with. She routinely spent hours obsessively cleaning the house, going from room to room to room, and then starting again. If we were making footprints on a carpet, she would walk behind us, vacuum in hand, erasing any evidence that we had been there.

Sometimes my dad would have a group of guys over to the house on a Sunday morning. They'd bring in bagels and shoot the shit. Without considering it intrusive, my mother would be right behind them with her vacuum, pushing it under their feet even as they talked. Why couldn't she wait until they left the house before she started cleaning? Perhaps it was her way of vacuuming up his shifty friends and his tawdry life.

CHAPTER FOUR

"How do you say 'ricotta'?"

One day, we went to Staten Island to look at houses. I was only seven. One minute we went there to look at real estate, and the next thing I knew, we were saying good-bye to Bensonhurst and heading west across the Verrazano-Narrows to the rural farmlands deep in the boonies of Staten Island.

I was very happy we were moving to the "burbs." I had only one good friend in Brooklyn, so I was too young to feel overly attached to my old neighborhood. To me, the move meant that we had made it, we were in the money. Our new house was even going to have plush wall-to-wall carpet, so I knew my mother would be a pig in mud with her vacuum.

We were leaving behind my aunt Diane, my mother's twin sister, and her new husband, Sandy, who was different from my father, not a street guy at all. But they knew where to find us if they wanted. And they did. They moved into the house attached to ours on Leggett Place. Their daughter, my cousin Gina, was just a baby at the time. My other cousin, Anthony, hadn't been born yet.

Everything about the move was exciting. My father bought all new furniture, so there were always trucks and moving men bringing in things like an enormous, new living room set still wrapped in plastic or bureaus and beds for the bedrooms. My bedroom was yellow and white, and I had a canopy bed outfitted with all new bedding in the style of a princess. My father built brick flower planters inside the house, trying to make the place fancy and special.

This first house on Staten Island was on Leggett Place, about three miles west of the Verrazano Bridge. The development was made up of new homes or homes that hadn't even been built yet. It was surrounded by farmland, but the best part was that there were a lot of younger families just starting out with kids around Gerard's and my age. Everything was done very communally. Gerard and I would watch out the window to see who was outside, and then we'd join the tons of other kids playing games and riding their bikes in the streets. All the mothers would hang out talking about current events, child issues, or meals, the favorite topics. If someone went in to cook dinner, the other moms on the street would watch out for anyone left. At night, after dinner, we'd all go into one another's basements and hang out until it was time for bed.

Most of the people in the neighborhood were Italian. In fact, a lot of them moved from Brooklyn to Staten Island, just like us. About a year after our arrival, I was so excited when my aunt Fran and uncle Eddie and my cousins, Lillian, Bud, Jerry, and Rena, moved in directly across the street. Dad told us that he wanted his sister to move there so she would be closer to us. Even my grandparents were moving in with them, to a small, attached apartment on the ground floor. I didn't know it then, but Uncle Eddie had lost his construction business. My father's parents had sold their Ronkonkoma house, which was their retirement home, to help bail him out. It killed my father that they had to sell their house and move in to help Eddie. Fran was family, and my dad was going to do whatever he had to do to take care of his sister. He made a thirty-thousand-dollar score and helped them move, get furniture, and get them out of their financial jam. My dad had to stop doing our own construction project and, for a while, our new furniture purchases were over. Luckily, the new beds had been some of the first things to arrive.

I liked that Eddie, Fran, and the rest of the Garafolas were across the street. We visited back and forth all the time. We had "our people" on the block now and had great times together. Initially, my father had been sad that his parents had to move just because of Eddie's situation. But it all worked out in the end. My grandparents seemed happy there, and after all, my father was my grandmother's baby, so being close to him was a bonus for her. When my grandfather died eight months later, my father was even more relieved that my grandmother had moved so much closer to us rather than being stuck in Ronkonkoma.

My brother, Gerard, loved food, so having relatives nearby who loved to feed him was perfection. He'd go over and eat a meal at Grandma's house, then he'd go to Aunt Fran's and eat there, and then he'd come home and eat at our house. But he'd tell everyone he hadn't eaten yet, so he'd get three meals out of the deal. Sometimes, from a farm behind the development, Gerard would steal a big squash or a tomato for my grandmother to put in her sauce. One time, the farmer was chasing Gerard down the block, telling him to bring back the stolen vegetables. Grandma was out there, too, screaming back at the farmer, "Don't you touch my grandson!" "He was stealing my vegetables!" the guy yelled back. But my grandmother prevailed, and both the squash and the tomato ended up in her sauce. It was delicious!

We all loved Grandma Kay. Having her across the street made it so easy to see her. She made the best sauce in the whole world. I was thirteen when she died. She hadn't been herself since my grandfather had passed away. She was really sad, and she started to get sick. She was the one who had originated my nickname, K.G., and for my thirteenth birthday she gave me a necklace with my initials in diamonds. Everybody got their initials in diamonds when they turned sixteen, so it was odd that I was getting mine at thirteen. She also bought me all of my china and silverware engraved with my initials for when I got married. She must have thought she wasn't going to make it three more years. The night before she died, we all went to the hospital to say good-bye. In the morning, she had passed away from a heart attack. Dad was sad, but he didn't harp on it.

Toniann was my best friend on Leggett Place. She lived two houses away. She was two years older than me, but that didn't bother either of us. We were in the same general age group, and we went to the same public school. Her parents both worked. Her father was a regular working guy, a nine-to-fiver, and her mother was a hairdresser. We used to sleep over at each other's houses all the time. We lost touch in our teenage years. I became a "bad" kid, sneaking out and going to nightclubs when I was fourteen. She didn't do stuff like that, so she hung out with the good kids while I regrouped with the ones who liked trouble.

I remember the one time Toniann made me so upset I almost cried. All Italians are very serious about their food, and we Gravanos were no exception. Toniann asked me to say the word "ricotta," so I complied and said the word exactly as she had said it, "ricotta." She responded with a hurtful taunt, "So *there*, you're *not* Italian! Italians say 'ree-*gut*.'" I was in disbelief. I knew I was Italian, and I couldn't even understand why she was challenging me. I pleaded my case. "You said to say 'ricotta' so I said 'ricotta.' If you had said, 'how do you say ricotta?' I would have said 'ree-*gut*.'" I may not have known my father was in the Mafia, but I knew I was as Italian as Cristobol Colon, even if I hadn't come over on the *Santa Maria* five hundred years earlier.

On Sundays, the whole family would go to Brooklyn to my mother's parents' house on Fifteenth Avenue and Eighty-sixth Street for church and dinner. Dad didn't go to church, but the rest of us would walk to St. Frances Cabrini on Eighty-sixth Street. After the service, Grandpa and I would walk to the Italian bakery and we'd get fresh bread and fresh mozzarella. Grandma would make us a huge Italian dinner of pasta and chicken and everything else. While she was cooking, Dad and I would go for our Sunday ritual of getting the car washed. He'd hand all the guys working there a nice tip after they'd polished it to look brand new.

Other days, he'd take me with him to the construction office, or even the social club once in a while. We were a team to be reckoned with, and I loved having him to myself.

My father was the only one in our neighborhood, Bulls Head, who was in the mob when we arrived on Staten Island. Our neighbors on Leggett Place all knew Dad was a gangster, but they didn't care. He had such people skills and was so normal and unpretentious that everybody liked him. He made everybody feel comfortable, just the opposite of the reaction you'd think they'd have. They knew his reputation as a tough guy, but that didn't affect how he was as a neighbor. He'd help anybody in any way he could. He wasn't exactly the handiest person, outside of specialty-carpentry, so if someone needed help with his car or mower, he'd tinker around a bit before calling someone else to help. He'd usually know the best person to call.

It was on Staten Island that my dad got back into the construction business. When Eddie went broke, he begged my father to bring him into "the life." My father understood that there was big money in construction, and he knew how to use his mob muscle to get the jobs, and he used his good work ethic to keep them coming. Uncle Eddie was the technical person, the nuts-and-bolts guy, who knew exactly how to get the construction done. He was good at making sure the crews were working and that they had all their necessary materials. Dad was good at being a gangster. I will admit, they made a good team. Dad got the jobs, and Uncle Eddie executed them.

Now that my father was back in the construction business, he and Paul Castellano had a lot more in common. Paul had been in control of the building industry in New York for the mob for quite some time. In fact, Paul, the *capo di tutticapi*, the boss of all bosses, had a stranglehold on anything concrete. If a project in New York City involved the pouring of cement, the man had a hand in it. My father was doing jobs for Paul, so now he was at the mansion on Todt Hill a lot.

Dad and Eddie's new business specialized in plumbing, and Paul was one of their first clients. Paul's house was so big that the water pressure fell off dramatically on the upper floors, so showering up there was very unpleasant. My father suggested installing a secondary station with an extra pump, and Paul was really happy with the result. Paul's affection for my father was sealed, and it wasn't long before he was throwing him and Eddie lots of work.

One time, my father brought me and my brother along with him to the mansion. The two men, my father and Paul, were going to talk business and we were along for the ride.

Paul's wife, Nina, answered the massive front door. She wasn't at all what I expected. I thought she'd be really dressed up, formal and fancy. Instead, she was unadorned and more like a grandmother, warm and welcoming. She stood barely five feet, her gray hair was neatly styled, and she wore a simple dress tailored below the knee. She brought Gerard and me into a kitchen bigger than our house. Dozens of shiny copper pots hung over a center island stove set in a pink marble countertop. A big ceiling fan circulated the aroma of freshly baking cookies, which she pulled from the oven. Gerard and I sat at the island eating cookies and drinking milk while our dad was otherwise disposed. We had never been inside a house like this, but living on Todt Hill was in our future.

We were still at Leggett Place when Dad decided he needed to unload The Plaza Suite, his most successful discotheque in Gravesend. Even though he loved running it, he had become so busy with the construction business, it was almost like he had two jobs. During the day, he worked at the construction office on the ground floor, below the discotheque. At night, the construction crews needed him for jobs, or so I thought. He couldn't be at the nightclub and out with the crew at the same time. He had two of his best guys, Mike DeBatt and Tommy

"Huck" Carbonaro, overseeing the operation, hoping that would let him keep it. However, when the Czech guy, Frank Fiala, made him the offer of a million dollars for the nightclub and building, Dad couldn't say no. It was five times the market value.

It wasn't until many years later that I finally learned the truth about what had happened between my father and Frank Fiala. Frank had put a hole through the wall of the construction office to connect it to the discotheque when he hadn't even anted up yet. My father was seething when he went to Brooklyn to confront him. When Dad got there, Fiala was sitting at my father's desk, surrounded by a pack of Doberman pinschers. My father already didn't like him, Fiala had a reputation as a showboater and a sleazy cocaine dealer. Dad demanded an explanation about the damage to the wall, and the guy pulled out an UZI and pointed it directly at my father's chest. My father gathered a couple of buddies up for retaliation.

All this happened around the time my family was getting ready to make the big move to Todt Hill. My father always seemed to have one foot in the door of a nicer house as soon as we settled anywhere. He loved construction and the challenge of upgrading a house. Paul Castellano living on the Hill didn't hurt. He liked proving himself by being a man with a manor, even though everyone loved living on Leggett Place. My mother had been dabbling in real estate a bit to keep busy, so she had a couple of affordable houses in the well-heeled neighborhood in mind.

CHAPTER FIVE

*"The cops were the bad guys. Why were
they doing this to us?"*

Todt Hill was the classiest neighborhood in Staten Island.
Almost everybody who lived there was a blue blood, although
there was some new money in the neighborhood, too. The lawyers, doctors, and bankers that kept New York City the capital
of the world lived in Todt Hill.

The English Tudor house where *The Godfather* was filmed
was in the neighborhood, sprawling, yes, but by no means one
of the biggest homes on the Hill. Paul Castellano's estate was
bigger, more extravagant, and more gorgeous by far. We moved
to Dad's own vision of a castle in the sky in 1982, when I was
eleven. We knew the neighborhood was stuffy before we got to
Todt Hill, but we figured we'd find a way to fit in.

My father was going to be completely hands-on in restoring
and expanding our new three-bedroom house on Buttonwood

Road to a five-bedroom showcase. He had bought the beautiful Victorian with a dark old-country interior, red velvet walls, and gorgeous French doors from the original owner, a woman in her eighties who was motivated to sell, but very particular about who she would sell to. She was captivated by my father's incomparable charm as he flattered her about her taste in interior design. He said he wasn't going to change a thing. First, he sweet-talked her so far down in the asking price she knocked off $100,000; then, when she thought we smelled like cigarette smoke, she said she'd only to sell to nonsmokers. My dad said it was the realtor who smoked, pointing to my mother. He swore himself a reformed man who had given up the nasty habit long ago. After that, every time my mother and he lit up a cigarette, he'd look around for a bolt of lightning that he was certain would strike him dead. I thought the place was not our style. It was old-fashioned and dark. My father pointed out that it was on a beautiful piece of property, nestled down in a little vale with tall trees all around it, giving it lots of privacy. He also reminded me he could turn the old place into a palace. And so he did.

The first thing he did after the closing was start sanding everything that could be sanded, the floors, moldings, and bannisters to lighten up the house. He hosted sanding parties where everybody we knew, including my mom, brother, and me, came to help sand. Dad's best friend, Stymie, and his family were there more than anybody. Stymie had recently sold his own house in Brooklyn to move to Lighthouse Hill, not far from Todt Hill, at my father's urging. Our two families were becoming really close. Stymie was like my own uncle and his kids were like my cousins. Stymie was also in the construction business and was almost as handy as my father. The two of them oversaw the installation of the state-of-the-art security system Dad desired. He was always conscious about security and personal safety. He had monitoring systems throughout the house and property.

Even before we moved to Todt Hill, I had started attending the exclusive private school there, Staten Island Academy. Dad said I was going to be a lawyer someday, so I needed to upgrade my education. "Knowledge is power," he would always tell me.

My mother would drive me from Leggett Place, which was four miles away on the back roads. She'd be wearing bell-bottom jeans and a sweatshirt, and she had very permed dark brown hair cut no longer than her shoulders. She'd be behind the wheel of her Ford Bronco in a long line of Mercedes-Benzes. The other moms would be very stylish and coiffed, wearing fur coats even if it was only for the morning drop-off. I was a little embarrassed that my mother was so Italian-homey. I begged her to try being a bit more fashionable, to wear a fur like the other mothers so she could fit in better. She told me to deal with it, she was who she was, and she wasn't going to change. She didn't care what other people thought about her. She had the fancy trappings in her closet. My father adored giving her furs and expensive jewelry, but she was a jeans-and-sneakers kind of person, so she left the furs in the closet and baubles home in the safe.

Unfortunately, I was not as self-confident back then. I had stopped hanging out with the old friends from Leggett Place to fit in with my new friends. The longer I lived on Todt Hill, the more desperately I wanted to be accepted by my classmates.

They were all members of one country club or another. I begged my dad to join the Richmond Country Club in order to be with my newer, richer friends over the summer break.

Dad balked at first, but eventually was agreeable to the idea. He grabbed one of his buddies, and we drove to the club in the Lincoln Town Car to find out about a membership. I spotted one of my girlfriends as soon as we entered the club-house and I hung out with her while Dad went into the office to talk about joining. I thought he looked a little out of place in his sweatsuit and pinky ring, but on the other hand, that was his style.

I was in the clubroom only about fifteen minutes when I heard the door to the office fly open and saw my father emerging, red-faced.

"Baby, let's get the fuck out of here!" he directed, waving his hand in the air for me to follow.

Embarrassed, I said a quick good-bye to my friend and rushed out after him. Climbing into the passenger seat of his big Lincoln, I waited for him to say something first.

"Karen, we're not joining. They're not our kind of people."

"But Daddy, everybody goes there. What am I going to do in the summer?"

"What's wrong with the country house?"

"I don't have any friends there, and it's so far away," I said.

"It's not that far, and I'll take you on a vacation, anywhere in the world you want to go."

I was disappointed, but I couldn't blame my father. During the ride home, he laughed about how the guy had asked for copies of his financials, proof of income. I assumed that meant we didn't make enough money to get into such a fancy place, and that wasn't his fault. It was only later that I realized our family had been denied membership because the club was prejudiced against gangsters.

In 1985, Dad was arrested. We were over at Aunt Fran's when we heard the news. The Feds had come to his office in Gravesend, and they'd taken both him and Uncle Eddie into custody. The police had been looking at Dad for three years, ever since Fiala's murder. But they couldn't get him on that charge. Even though the police were pretty sure Dad was involved, the detectives could not gather enough information, so the investigation went nowhere. Everyone in the neighborhood knew what had happened, but no one ever told on my father.

The cops couldn't get him, but the Feds did. They indicted him and my uncle on money laundering and tax evasion charges related to the sale of The Plaza Suite. As part of the investigation, the Feds even raided our farm in New Jersey, which was like our heaven.

Up until that point, our neighbors in Cream Ridge really didn't know who Dad was. Sure, they thought he was different, shady perhaps, but they didn't really know he was this ambitious gangster, Sammy the Bull. They just knew him as "Sammy."

I suspected my father had likely played a role in Fiala's demise. Still, I found myself feeling bad for him. He was under tremendous stress because of all the heat coming down on him. Years later we would have to sell the farm at Cream Ridge to pay the three-hundred-thousand-dollar tax bill Dad owed the IRS. Even though it sounds crazy, seeing my father so upset made me feel like the cops were the bad guys. Why were they doing this to us?

The day before Dad learned he beat the rap on the tax evasion charges, his best friend Stymie was gunned down at Tali's, a bar that my father and Stymie owned together. What should have been a time of celebration was now marred by the loss of his closest friend. The Colombo associate who killed him was drunk and high, and out celebrating the fact he was about to be "made." Stymie died honorably, protecting the female bartender who was being harassed by the bastard. Everybody in our family was devastated. Stymie was family to us. He and Dad had redone our Todt Hill house together.

I went to the funeral. It was weird how many people were specifically giving my father their respects and condolences. They were saying, "Sammy, I'm sorry." Why were they paying *him* respect? That's not his brother, I thought. Why was everyone going over to my dad before offering condolences to Stymie's *wife*? That's when I started looking at it and saying my dad must be the boss here. He was definitely the boss of everything here. When my father had been "made," he got his own crew. The crew was like our family. We went on vacations together. Stymie had been closest to Dad, but the whole crew was in mourning when he died. There were Louis Milito, "Old Man" Paruda, and Thomas "Huck" Carbonaro, all in a state despair. This was the only time I ever saw my father cry. I saw him in the kitchen when he came downstairs after the funeral. I saw a single tear. That was it.

CHAPTER SIX

"If I do get killed, I want you to go on living
every day like you do today."

In December of 1985, Paul Castellano was murdered along with his bodyguard at Sparks Steak House in New York City. The story was the featured splash on the evening news. I was in my bedroom, only half paying attention to the television I'd gotten for my birthday, when I heard one of the female newscasters detailing Castellano's rubout live from the scene on East Forty-sixth Street between Second and Third Avenues.

I remembered the first time I had ever seen Paul Castellano. I had been crouched in the window of my aunt Fran's bedroom back on Leggett Place. Dad would always send us across the street to Aunt Fran's house whenever he was hosting a meeting that he didn't want us to be around for. That night, as my mother, brother, and aunt sat around the kitchen table, I had snuck upstairs to Aunt Fran's room to spy on our house. I had watched in awe as big black cars pulled up in front and men in suits strode up our walkway. One man in particular had caught my attention. He was an older gentleman with combed gray hair, tall and impeccably dressed. I knew instantly that he was Dad's boss, Paul Castellano.

When I returned home the next morning, I found a platter of leftover cannolis on the table in a room that was off-limits to us even on holidays, the "museum dining room." I knew something really important had taken place the night before. I imagined my father hosting a secret induction meeting, having someone "made." I recently learned the real story when I visited him in prison. The meeting had been about the murder of Philadelphia crime boss Angelo Bruno. The Philadelphia people had wanted to have a meeting with Paul Castellano so they could gain favor with the Gambino family, and my father had hosted the gathering. I never had enough courage to ask my father any questions about secret stuff growing up. But I knew and respected the code, "mind your business and don't ask."

Now, as I was watching the newscast with the bullet-riddled bodies of Paul Castellano and his underboss covered by blankets in the background, I knew full well that Castellano was my father's boss in the construction business. I flew down to the kitchen to see if Dad was anywhere around. I was calm almost in a weird way, like murder had been accepted in my life. It was becoming something easier for me to deal with, but I was nevertheless concerned for Dad's safety. When I reached the kitchen, Mom was standing at the stove preparing dinner.

"Do you think Daddy knows about Paul?" I blurted out in fear, thinking I already knew the answer.

"I'm sure he does," she said in a calm, reassuring voice. "It's all over the news."

It was getting harder and harder for me to buy into my mother's easy assurances. Paul was the second person close to my father to be gunned down in the last nine months. First Stymie, now Paul.

My father didn't come home after Castellano died. He was gone for more than two weeks. He was holed up in a safehouse with Frankie DeCicco, now the underboss, but I didn't know it. I thought maybe he was on vacation in Florida. I had no idea who he was with. But I knew it was not with Uncle Eddie because he had been stopping in regularly to check on me, Mom, and Gerard. My mother gave me the usual reassuring brush-offs, but no information about where Dad had gone or when he was coming back.

I was concerned that something might have happened to him. But I tried not to think about it. I had a way of blocking things out. Maybe it was because, when I was a kid, Dad had always made me feel everything would be okay, and I believed him. I felt that no matter what, he would always be okay. Even so, I couldn't help but worry every now and then. I was too terrified to even think about the obvious, that Dad was off avenging Paul's murder, or worse, that Dad was involved. From my bedroom I could hear the garage door when it opened. Every night I would lie awake, hoping to hear his car coming in.

I couldn't get the image of Paul Castellano lying in the street in a pool of blood out of my mind. I'd worry that that same thing had happened to my father. Uncle Nicky, my mother's brother, had just "disappeared" when I was six. His body was never found, but I did overhear a family member say that his hand had been recovered. I was so devastated by my uncle's death that I completely blocked it from my mind and refused to think that another tragedy would ever happen to my family again. But I took only small comfort in that. The entire Scibetta family was devastated at the loss of Uncle Nicky, especially my grandmother.

Finally, my father turned up in our kitchen early one morning. There was a newspaper folded under his arm, which he casually dropped on the table.

"Sit down," he said, opening up the *New York Daily News*. I saw a picture of my dad and I knew right away, he was showing me a story about the slaughter of Paul Castellano.

"I want you to read it," he said.

My father stood over me while I skimmed the article, filled with gory details I wanted to know but had known not to ask about before.

The story identified Sammy Gravano as a "rising star in the mafia," calling him a hit man with the Gambino crime family, the most powerful of New York's five organized crime families. The article said John Gotti was Sammy's boss and that Sammy was considered to be one of the people moving up the ladder into a top position within the family. Now that Castellano had been killed, the family was under new leadership and there were a lot of power plays going on and people were shifting their roles. I had never heard John Gotti's name before.

"Do you believe everything you read?" my dad asked when I finally looked up.

I shrugged my shoulders and said I didn't know if I did or not.

Leaning forward, he looked me in the eyes and said, "There is some truth in there." He didn't get into detail. "Don't think you can't ever come to me with a question. There are some things I can answer and some things I can't because they're my business."

At fourteen, these were the adolescent issues I had to digest, what kind of sinister underworld my family inhabited. While other girls were worrying about clothes, their bra size, their schoolwork, and boys, I was trying to wrap my head around "murder incorporated."

In the next few months, I noticed my father was commanding an even higher level of respect. People were shaking his hand, his crew around him got tighter, he got a driver, and he dramatically upgraded his wardrobe. I saw the transformation right away with my father going shopping for shirts and ties at a store on Eighteenth Avenue in Brooklyn. He had to get dressed up to go and meet John Gotti. He had to start playing the role of consigliere, third in command. There were the flashy ties that he came home with. I remember thinking they were John Gotti ties because they were red and black and flamboyant. My father didn't like to get dressed up, but he came home from the store with ten suits. He liked to stay fit and work out. He was into boxing, he ate right, and he didn't put salt on his food. He wanted us all to be more health conscious, too.

I liked his new look. I thought he looked good. I told him, "This is the way you should dress, Dad. I think you look good." He just smiled. I think it made him feel good, but I don't think he paid much attention to what I said. My father really didn't care much about personal style, he was more concerned about his new role in the Gambino family.

Now when my construction-company-owner father went out

for meetings with the "boss," he got dressed up in designer suits and silk ties. My father's signature sweatsuits and sneakers apparently were not acceptable for someone in his new position. Dad wasn't the only one being treated special. The whole family was getting the red carpet treatment. When we went out to dinner, way more often than we used to, we were picked up by a driver in a Lincoln Town Car. The maître d' would greet us by name and bring us to a prized table.

When we visited Aunt Fran and Uncle Eddie in Bulls Head, we were like celebrities. The kids would point and whisper, "That's Sammy's daughter." They didn't shy away from me, so I figured they were envious. I liked all the newfound attention, I felt special. Everyone in that neighborhood seemed to want to be a gangster. They were obsessed with the high-profile Castellano hit, so sensational it almost seemed out of Hollywood. There was talk that my father was responsible. But had he really killed someone at the heart of rush hour and gotten away with it?

I knew my family was different, but we were still a family. We had a nice house in Todt Hill and spent summers at the farm in the country until the place was sold, playing checkers on family game night. Anyone from the outside who looked at our family without knowing our name assumed that we were the typical American household.

My father went to work like any other father, even if being a mob lieutenant was a rather unusual career. The "company" was headed by John Gotti. I had never heard of him until Paul Castellano had been murdered. Now Dad was his chief confidant and protector. If you wanted to get face time with John Gotti, you had to go through my father. He gave the thumbs-up or the thumbs-down as to who would go through the door. My father ran the construction part of the enterprise, but John was the king who sat on the throne. Dad was really big in construction. He outshined the entire Gambino family in that venture. He was building all over the city.

Frankie DeCicco was the next casualty from Dad's group of friends. Frankie was not in my father's crew. He had his own crew and was very powerful in the Gambino family. When my father agreed to take out Paul, he wanted Frankie to be the boss, because he felt that Frankie would be a better boss than John. My father and Frankie were very close. Both men were good earners, very dangerous, and very respected not only within the Gambino family, but by other crime families as well. Frankie thought that John's ego was too big and that it would be better for him to be the underboss for the time being. If John was not doing a good job, he would reconsider taking his place, when the time was right. But that time never came. Frankie had told my father that because the hit on Paul was not sanctioned, the other crime families would more than likely try to retaliate against them.

Only the Mafia Commission could authorize the assassination of a boss. True to the Mafia code, a hit was put out on the men believed to be responsible for killing Paul. Genovese family crime boss Vincent "The Chin" Gigante, who was also the head of the Mafia Commission, ordered a hit on Frankie and John Gotti and others they felt were responsible. Someone had to pay for the violation of the code when Castellano was killed.

This time, I was with Mom at Aunt Diane's house when I heard the news that Frankie, who was identified as the Gambino family underboss, was blown up in a car outside of a club in Brooklyn, and another man was injured. I knew that Frankie and my Dad had been riding together to Brooklyn to meet John. But it wasn't until I heard it on the news that I learned that they had gone to the Veterans & Friends Social Club in Dyker Heights. I feared the person who had been injured when DeCicco was killed in the car explosion had to be my father. I ran upstairs to find my mother, who was in the master bedroom talking to her sister.

"Mom, is Daddy okay?" I begged.

"Yes, he's fine," she said, crying. I'd seen her cry when Stymie died. "He's on his way home. He's just very, very upset about Frankie." She said she couldn't believe it. She had known the DeCicco family from Bensonhurst since she was a kid.

Holy crap, I started thinking. *What is this life?* I looked at it and at everything the people looked up to. I didn't know if I wanted to grow up wondering every day if something was going to happen to my father. *Was this life really worth it?*

Mom and I were home by the time Dad got there. I started crying when I saw him. I hugged him, and he kissed me on the forehead and hugged me back. He went into the bedroom to take a shower and clean up a little.

I heard that he had been there for the explosion. The bomb had been intended for John, but the assassin had detonated it prematurely, mistaking another guy who was there for Gotti. My father had tried to pull Frankie's lifeless body away from the burning car. The whole body felt like all the fluid had drained out of it. My father grabbed ahold of what he thought was Frankie, but ended up with only two detached body parts, a leg and an arm.

When Dad got out of the shower, I asked him, "Is there any way that you could possibly die or get killed?"

He answered me, "Yes. If I do get killed, I want you to go on living every day like you do today. I want you to be strong for your mother. I want you to help guide your brother, and I want you to understand that this is the life I chose. And this is why it's so important to me for you and your brother to go to school and make a different life for yourselves.

"I love you, and I don't want you to worry every day about me. I'll be okay."

He was clearly upset. He had been very close to Frankie, but it was part of business. When I was a kid he was able to pat my head and shrug it off. He didn't have to answer me, but he did have enough respect for me to tell me what he could. He was aware that I had known these men since the time I was a little girl. They were like family to me. He also knew that no matter how much he tried to shield me from his world, I was a part of it. He knew I worried about him. Mom and Dad went to Frankie's funeral, but I didn't go.

After Frankie's death, Dad was promoted to Number Two, the underboss.

Dad's notoriety had an enormous downside. Apparently, the people on the Hill and our friends in Bulls Head differed in their opinion of my father's Mafia status. The Bulls Headers thought Dad was a celebrity and cool; the Todt Hillers thought he was a pariah and objectionable. What they thought of him spilled over onto what they thought of everyone in our family. Gerard was the first one to experience the rejection.

He never really liked living in Todt Hill. When he was nine or ten, he and some of his friends were playing with fire-crackers in an area of Todt Hill where a couple of new homes were being built. Some leaves caught fire, and Gerard was blamed.

A couple of years later, when my father's picture was frequently in the paper for the wrong reasons, my brother had been hanging around the house looking bored. Mom suggested he go outside and play with one of the kids on the road, a boy about Gerard's age, just a few houses down, named David.

"David said he's not allowed to play with me 'cause Daddy's a gangster," Gerard told her.

My mother was so insulted. When she confronted David's mother, the woman repeated the sentiment. "We don't raise our kids like that," she told Mom. By the way she was acting, my mother could tell that she didn't want her kids to play with Gerard. She was one of those people who thought she was better than everyone else, a socialite. I am sure in her eyes a gangster's kid did not make a good playmate for her son.

After that, Mom told my father she wanted to move back to Bulls Head. "You know, Sammy, I don't think we should live here anymore," I overheard her telling Dad. "I don't feel like we fit in here, with all these people driving around in fancy cars wearing furs. That's not me."

Dad wanted to make her feel better, so he agreed. He accepted the fact that he was a gangster, so he wanted us to go around with our heads held high. I think he was just as ready to leave as Mom was. Todt Hill wasn't our thing. My father loved the house, but he sympathized with her and felt we didn't fit in there.

There was also another reason we needed to move. With Paul Castellano and Frankie dead, the chances of my father taking a bullet had risen dramatically. Our house was very accessible to anybody; it had too many windows, was surrounded by trees, and was on a very narrow street. Anyone who wanted to get to my father could do it easily and get out without being seen. He accepted that he might die, but he wanted to be sure my mother was living in the neighborhood she loved before anything happened to him. He was very cautious. He was a hit man before becoming the underboss, so he understood every aspect of this life. He was always on alert. And always drove slowly down Buttonwood to Willow Pond, making a left on Todt Hill Road, and coming back along Circle Road a couple of times before coming back to the house.

I was defiant about leaving Todt Hill. I did not want to relocate again. "I don't want to move!" I bellowed. "Why do we have to?" The next thing I knew, we were about to close on a property on Lamberts Lane, only a few blocks from our old house on Leggett Place. When Dad took me to see the house, I nearly cried. It was a puke green Cape right on the service road of the Staten Island Expressway. The place was so small and square it looked like a Monopoly piece taken from the board and plunked straight down on Mediterranean Avenue or Baltic Avenue, the cheapest properties of the game.

"Are you crazy?" I protested. "I don't want to live in that house." Dad smiled, and then ordered me out of the car. The interior of the place was even worse. It had not been updated in a century and had two small bedrooms with sloped ceilings, clearly carved out of a space that had once been the attic.

"Don't worry. It's not gonna look like this when I'm done with it." He basically blew out all but one wall, and remodeled the tiny ranch from three bedrooms into a gorgeous three-level house, complete with a gorgeous in-ground pool, that became the talk of the neighborhood. The house had only three bedrooms, but the rooms were huge and all of them had their own bathrooms. I had my very own sitting room, so when all of my friends came over we would be comfortable. My father wanted the house to be perfect, and he wanted to make it a place where Gerard and I wanted to hang out and bring our friends. If our accommodations were comfortable, Gerard and I would spend more time at home and out of trouble.

It was so funny. Dad was always talking about fitting in and keeping a low profile, but then he would turn an ordinary house into an eyepopper, defeating the whole purpose. Ours was the nicest house in Bulls Head, with great details and extra touches, and everyone was whispering, "Sammy the Bull just moved in." Because the neighborhood was predominantly Italian, being a gangster was a good thing.

The house on the unadorned corner lot had been hideous, but it was all about location, location, location. The house was situated exactly at one of the loop ramp entrances for the eastbound Staten Island Expressway, making it virtually impossible for anyone in a car, be it a hit man or a cop, to covertly loiter or park in the area. Any car in front of our house was forced into the flow of traffic onto the freeway. Just as important, it was a great escape route for anybody inside our house who needed to suddenly hightail it away. The security was tight throughout the property. For anyone who thought going around the corner to the next street was an option, my father had built a massive brick wall along the side that faced Seldin Avenue and along the backyard.

Once again, this was *Sammy's house,* and everything was top shelf. He had telephones installed in every room, even the bathrooms. He took charge of all the tasks, from being the site planner to the builder. He even worked hands-on with the interior designer he hired. He should have been an architect, so exact was his vision of how something should look and where an element should go.

For Lamberts Lane, my father hired a well-respected, well-known landscape architect to work with him on the grounds. My father had an appointment with him, even though we hadn't moved in yet. Dad wanted the place to be perfect for our arrival. Both Dad and the landscape architect were very excited, because my father had a very big vision and a big budget, and what landscape designer doesn't like that in a client? I was there with Dad on the day the guy arrived in high spirits to show my father the renderings and present him with the plans and to assess drainage and terrain issues.

My father was excited, and while we waited for the landscape designer, he showed me where this and that tree were going to go, and described how they'd look in the different seasons. His business associates, Uncle Eddie, Huck, and some of the other guys in Dad's crew, were there for the big unveiling. The architect brought out huge rolls of schematics covered with diagrams and layovers with every kind of option. Finally, it came time to roll out the bottom line.

All of a sudden, the mood changed. My father looked at the sheet with the estimate, then looked at the poor guy with fire in his eyes. "Karen, go inside," he ordered me abruptly. I went in hesitantly, but took a spot by the window where I could watch and hear everything.

"You're fucking kidding me, right?" I heard Dad bellow at the startled man. I could see the guy starting to get really scared. He was backpedaling and justifying the best he could.

"Well, Sammy," he explained, "we are pulling this tree out

of upstate, and that tree has to be imported from some other part of the country, and that other tree is a hybrid," and so he continued.

My father was livid. "Are you fucking *kidding* me? I should fucking kill you right now, right here! Are you fucking trying to *rob me?*" he kept repeating. The architect was terrified. When my father got hot and bothered, everybody was terrified. I could see the architect sitting on the windowsill crying and begging for his life. My father wound up taking the architect's plans and ripping them into pieces. They eventually found a compromise, cutting back on some of the more expensive elements and replacing them with other trees, but one thing the man learned which I already knew, do *not* try to rip off Sammy the Bull.

My father was very fair when it came to the bottom line, and he expected the people he dealt with to be honest and reasonable as well. The landscape architect was taking advantage of him, not knowing how much he paid attention to the cost details. Just because he had deep pockets, didn't mean he was an extravagant spender. My father was completely unaware of how much his highfalutin design plan would realistically cost. I don't think he realized how expensive a single tree could be, so both men were at fault. Dad was not a man who spent a lot of money on clothes, but he spared no expense when it came to his homes. However, the second you tried to rip him off, most likely you'd regret it. He was very generous when it came to numbers, but he was also a man who knew the value of a dollar, and he didn't want to be taken advantage of. Even now, from prison, he watches the bottom line for me, making sure no one is trying to screw me over.

CHAPTER SEVEN

"Say hello to your uncle John."

The first time I encountered John Gotti was when he called the house to talk to Dad not long after Paul Castellano was gunned down. I answered the phone and the male on the other end said, "Who's this?"

I answered, "Karen," and the man said, "Hey Karen, this is your uncle John. Is your father home?"

I knew this was the person I had seen so many times in the papers and on the news after Paul died. He intrigued me, with his dapper confidence and swagger. He was like a movie star to me, a celebrity. He rode in shiny Lincoln Town Cars and had a crew of men around him. He reeked of importance.

From that phone call forward, John was in Dad's life. If John needed something, my father would jump. It just seemed like everything got more formal. We used to eat dinner as a family every night at 5:30 P.M. Now Dad had to eat dinner at 5:00 because he had to meet John at the social club on Mulberry Street in Little Italy at 6:00.

That's when I became "Sammy's daughter," but it was bigger than that. The transformation in how my father was received went from straight-up respect, to respect coupled with fear. This was the first time I saw that people were afraid of him, that he was powerful, and that he controlled something. From the moment Paul Castellano was killed, my father was in the spotlight with John. He was the guy carrying the umbrella while John was walking down the street. He was the second in command and helping to run the most powerful crime family in New York.

The first time I met John Gotti was at my Sweet Sixteen party. I had seen him at my father's office on Stillwell Avenue a couple of times, but this was the first time we were introduced. The celebration was at Pastels in Brooklyn, a well-known Mafia hangout. For the big occasion, I wore a pink leather dress, custom made. It was really tight-fitting, had a sweetheart top and came with a matching pink leather jacket. I complimented the ensemble with pink high heels. I got my hair professionally styled and it was teased and sprayed to the max. My father forewarned me that John was going to be there. "When you meet John, you be polite. You mind your manners," he told me.

Fifty teenagers and sixty men with their families were at the party. My fifty friends included cousins, classmates from Staten Island Academy, and schoolyard guy friends from Leggett Place. Dad's sixty men friends were all wiseguys.

Dad hired a DJ who played songs I chose personally and a video-photographer. I didn't realize the photographer stank until after the party was over, and I was watching the video with friends. All the footage was shot on the dance floor, nothing else. I complained to Dad, who told me that was how it had to be. My father had told the guy not to come up past the sunken dance floor where the tables were to keep him from filming the top wiseguys who were in attendance. In the middle of the festivities, there was a whisper circulating in the crowd. "John Gotti's here," my classmates were murmuring excitedly. It was as if I had a celebrity at my Sweet Sixteen. My father brought John over to the bar, where I was hanging out with some of my friends, and said, "Say hello to your uncle John."

I didn't even have an uncle named John. I kissed him on the cheek. The Don smiled, congratulated me on getting older, and handed me an envelope stuffed with ten crisp one-hundred-dollar bills.

He was totally different from my dad. He was serious and poised, not the least bit warm and bubbly. He was not the "hey kiddo" type, he was very serious. He needed to be catered to and worshipped. I minded my manners, like my father had told me. But I was relieved when he exited to a back room where all the wiseguys were hanging out.

A couple of days later, there was a note taped to my locker at school. It said, "I heard you had a nice Sweet Sixteen. Must be nice to be a Mafia princess." It wasn't signed. I thought it might be from a girl whose boyfriend liked me, but I was not sure. I also didn't know if it was meant as a compliment or an insult. I never felt like I was a Mafia princess. I felt like my father was a kingpin among gangsters, but the "royalty" thing began and ended there.

I never felt completely comfortable at Staten Island Academy. I would dress up like the other kids, walk around with Fendi bags and such, but I always felt different.

When I was twelve, somebody gave my dad a Gucci bag, which he passed on to me. I thought the thing was hideous and told him I didn't want it. He told me, "It's from Italy. It's supposed to be nice." A couple of years went by, and all my friends were carrying Gucci bags. I asked my mother what became of mine.

"I thought you didn't like it," she said. She told me she had given it away.

"Now I need to have it," I said in my best convincing voice. "Everyone at school has one."

"Guess what? You're not getting one now," said my mother. "You don't need something because everyone else has it. You get something because *you* want it."

So I went to the school locker room the next day and stole someone's Gucci bag.

Dad asked how I got a Gucci bag. He knew my mom had given away the one I didn't like, so I told him.

"Unbelievable. Now what are you gonna do?" He knew I couldn't walk around the school with stolen property, especially since someone at the school was looking for it.

Dad ordered me to get rid of it. In a sense, I think, deep down inside, my father secretly liked that I was a lot like him, and if I wanted something I knew how to get it. But, on the other hand, he did not want me robbing and stealing. That was not how he wanted his kids to be.

I snuck it back into the locker room the next morning, and Dad bought me the Gucci bag of my choice.

At the end of the day, when all was said and done, I wasn't used to going to country clubs, having nannies, and going to summer camp. That wasn't who I was. Deep down inside, I always kind of knew I could fit in, go with the flow, try to make it work at Staten Island Academy. Now, at sixteen, I just plain didn't want to. People now knew who my father was. I kind of felt like it was cool. Everybody else thought it was cool, and it made my Mafia connection more accepted. "It is what it is," I told myself.

Maybe I was on a little high, intrigued about Dad's notoriety. My father was on the front page of newspapers and it seemed surreal. It felt as though my dad were two different people, Sammy the Bull to the world, and an affectionate, fun-loving father to me.

After Paul was killed and my father aligned himself with John Gotti, I attached myself more than ever to the people I felt comfortable with, all of whom had mob connections. I liked Dina Milito, Dad's friend Louie's daughter, and Dori LaForte, whose grandfather was a bigwig in the Gambino family. Dori was two years older than me, but it didn't matter to either of us. We were like the little Italian gangster girls. Although we didn't act like that, we felt that way. We knew who and what our fathers were, but we never talked about it.

I convinced my parents that Staten Island Academy was not for me. I felt that I had outgrown the school. I wanted a change and talked my parents into letting me switch schools to be with girls who were more like me. I'd still go to parties hosted by the school, but I stopped being invited to my classmates' houses. I didn't care. I was becoming less interested in the kids at the house parties and more interested in the kids who were hanging out on the street corners and in the schoolyards. I got Mom and Dad's blessing to transfer to Richmondtown Prep School on Richmond Road. It wasn't that far from Lamberts

Lane, and Roxanne and Ramona Rizzo went there. They were Dad's friend Johnny Rizzo's daughters, but we were lifelong friends. Johnny's father, "Old Man Rizzo," was a captain in the Gambino crime family. My father had been a member of his crew when he first came over from the Colombo crime family. Johnny and my father grew up together. The girls' maternal grandfather was Benjamin "Lefty Guns" Ruggiero, a soldier in the Bonanno crime family, who was portrayed by Al Pacino in the 1997 movie *Donnie Brasco*. Ramona and I were a month apart in age, but I hung out more with Roxanne, who was a year younger than me.

We had been very close since we were little kids. We were so tight, we were always at each other's houses growing up. We even called each other cousin. We had drifted apart when I went to Staten Island Academy, but we started to hang out again at Richmondtown Prep, and I was ready to get back together with my old friends.

Gerard was still struggling along. He had been going to the public school, Intermediate School 72, but I wanted him to go to school with me. I convinced my parents that Richmondtown Prep was a school for kids who don't get along in other schools, so they'd be agreeable. After he was enrolled, my parents were so pissed that I had conned them. It was okay, though. The school was so laid back and small. It was pretty much run by a family. Mr. White was the dean; Miss White was the teacher, and Mrs. White was everybody else.

My brother was the quiet kid, even though he was very mischievous. He was severely dyslexic, like my dad. My mother would cry and pull her hair out trying to help him. He was always in outreach classes and he had to have tutors at the house. He'd act out at school a lot, too. He had been held back in first grade. It wasn't until he went to private school that we found out what was really wrong with him.

My mother was extremely protective of Gerard. She didn't want to admit that he had dyslexia, and she enabled him by doing his schoolwork for him. At school, he would do weird stuff like go to the bathroom and never return to class, or start fights like my father had done when he had trouble in school.

My father had told me about his struggles in school. He had been red-flagged as a slow learner because of his dyslexia. Back then, dyslexia was not understood, let alone recognized as a disability. My father dropped out of school in the eighth grade rather than endure the mockery he was subjected to from teachers and fellow classmates alike.

When teachers told Dad that Gerard was dyslexic, he was heartbroken. He did everything within his means to help his son overcome the disability. He hired specialists, tutors, and doctors to take on the challenge. Still, he was very hard on Gerard, pushing him to do better. He didn't want Gerard to follow in his footsteps. He wanted Gerard to be far away from the life.

I remembered one time, in particular, when Dad practically terrorized the poor kid. We had an in-ground pool in our backyard on Lamberts Lane, which attracted a lot of pigeons. They landed on the patio area and did their pooping there. Dad hated the annoying, messy birds with a passion. He ran inside, grabbed a BB gun, and started shooting them one by one. Gerard was about thirteen years old at the time. He was horrified watching the dead birds drop out of the sky onto the cement, although he was trying not to show it. When my father handed him the rifle and said it was his turn, he froze up. "Shoot!" my father ordered. Gerard didn't want Dad to perceive him as a coward, so he aimed and fired. He succeeded in hitting the bird, but not killing it. It was screaming and writhing in pain on the patio.

"Kill the fucking thing!" my father directed.

Gerard just stood there, paralyzed. He loved animals, so he couldn't bear to watch the bird suffer. But at the same time he couldn't bring himself to pull the trigger a second time.

Grabbing the rifle, my father quickly took care of business and put the bird out of its misery. "It's okay, Son," he said, patting Gerard sympathetically on the shoulder. He was kind that way, but he always said Gerard was "not cut out for the life." I was the survivor. If Dad had handed me the gun that day, I would have killed sixty pigeons. I was the girl, though, so it wasn't expected of me.

Gerard was a really good kid outside of school. He never talked back to my parents. He was so obedient. If my parents said to be home at a certain time, he was home right at that time. I was the rebel, not Gerard.

One time, my friend Jackie and I stole clothes out of our classmate Lisa Bongiorno's locker at school. We went to Jackie's, and she put on the clothes we had just stolen. The doorbell rang, and Jackie opened the door. There was Lisa Bongiorno standing in the doorway. "Nice outfit," she said.

I just closed the door in her face. "Oh my God, we are in trouble," I told Jackie.

Lisa went back to the school and told the principal.

I went home, knowing how much trouble we were in.

I found my father in the kitchen, "I have to tell you something," I said. "Today Jackie and I stole clothes from a locker and the girl we stole them from came to Jackie's house and saw Jackie wearing them. She told the principal and we are probably going to get in trouble."

"So what are you going to do about it?" my father wanted to know.

"I don't know," I said. "But I am worried that I might get expelled." I was thinking that my answer to Dad's question should have been "tell the truth." I didn't want to tell the truth, but I felt that was the correct response. "I don't know" was all I said.

"Well, here's what you are going to do," Dad instructed. "You're going say, 'I don't know how the clothes got there.' Then you are going to take the consequences, whatever they may be." If I admitted my role, then I was also admitting Jackie's guilt.

"So I'm not in trouble?" I asked.

"Oh, you are in trouble for stealing, but that's with me. I am going to deal with you."

My father made me go to school. When the principal asked me about the clothes, I said I didn't know anything.

I had in-school suspension for a week. I had to sit in the dean's office and do my homework. Jackie and I had to apologize to Lisa when we gave her the clothes back.

My father's punishment to me was that I had to wash and iron all of his clothes, and I had to do chores around the house for a week. The ratting lesson was you had to stand behind what you did. No matter what the consequences were, you were not going to rat.

CHAPTER EIGHT

"You cannot be crawling off my roof at night."

I loved sneaking out of our house at night. When Dad remodeled the house on Lamberts Lane, he gave Gerard and me the bedrooms at the top of the stairs. When you walked in, the staircase was right there. At the top of the stairs, if you went to the left it was Gerard's room and to the right was my room. I had my own bathroom and my own sitting area, so a lot of my friends wanted to be at my house. We were out of the way upstairs, and Dad made it like that to keep us close. He kept his bedroom downstairs.

The fact that his bedroom was at the bottom of the stairs didn't help. We'd go in my bathroom, undo the window, and crawl out. Then, we'd walk along the roof of the first floor, which took us over the kitchen. Sometimes, Dad, Mom, or both of them would be in there, and we'd have to walk really quietly. That roof went a long ways, but eventually we'd be at the end. The jump-off point was near our glassed-in den, with big glass doors that looked out onto the backyard and the pool. Most of the time, all that glass didn't matter, because at night my parents wouldn't be in there. They'd be in their bedroom with the TV on. Plus, Dad had so carefully insulated every ceiling and rafter that it made the best escape route ever.

If my parents were awake, we'd jump down onto the fence and then into the neighbors' yard. If they were already asleep, we'd just jump into our yard and sneak out the side door to the sidewalk. We'd go over to the P.S. 60 schoolyard, where a bunch of gangster thugs in the making would be hanging out.

There was always something going on there. Kids would be stealing cars, having fights. That was the place where all the Springville boys from Staten Island hung out. The Springville boys had the reputation of being the gangster wannabes of the Staten Island teenage population, and they honored their reputation admirably.

They were kind of like the Rampers, Dad's first gang in Brooklyn, but there were more of them. They were from the Bulls Head and Springville neighborhoods on Staten Island.

They were trying to make their bones in the streets with the hopes of someday catching the eye of a made guy from some crime family. They really did not want to be part of that life. They wanted to be on their own, but they would quickly learn that if they wanted to be running the streets, they would have to follow the code. The difference between my father and them was that most of them really didn't understand what the Mafia stood for. They looked at it more for the money and notoriety than the honor, loyalty, and brotherhood that the old-timers practiced. A lot of them ended up going to jail for petty crimes.

There was one guy at the schoolyard named Tommy who I thought was cute. The first time I actually talked to him was during my father's annual Fourth of July party at our house. Dad always threw the biggest party in Bulls Head for the celebration, with garbage pails full of Dom Pérignon, alcohol, beer, lobster tails, crab legs, anything you could want. Hundreds of people from all over the neighborhood came to the event. People would bring their lawn chairs and set them up out in the yard. We just let people come in, anyone who wanted. It was a replica of the huge Fourth of July event that John Gotti always had in Queens.

By mid-afternoon, all the adults were drunk and wasted. Roxanne, Ramona, and I had left the party for a little walk when I saw Tommy in his car waiting for some friends. I had seen him around the neighborhood, and I liked him. When he told me he was going to a block party, I said, "That's my family's party."

He walked back to the house with us and as we were walking into the backyard, I saw my cousin Bud running with my father's friend, Sera, who was carrying a bloodied and beat-up teenager. Bud was yelling, "Get the fuck outta here and don't come back!"

I was horrified when Bud next walked over to Tommy and asked if he knew the kid. Tommy said he had never seen him before. I was so embarrassed, I went to find my mother.

"Mom, what's going on?" I asked her.

She was as drunk as everybody else. I had never seen her with a drink before, let alone drunk. "Don't worry, Karen, just chill out," she advised me. So I went to find my dad.

"Dad, what happened?" I asked him.

"Apparently some kid mouthed off and he got a beating," he

told me. It turned out he was some kid from the schoolyard. He had gotten drunk at the party and grabbed someone's ass. Someone else at the party saw it and said, "Buddy, we don't do that here." The kid mouthed off back, and wound up getting roughed up for being disrespectful.

Tommy was still following me around, so I introduced him to my father. "Dad, this is Tommy," I said. Dad must have thought I was dating him the way he sized him up.

"Tommy, I'm gonna tell you right now," my father said. "If you start a problem, you're gonna leave the same way." Dad probably said it to test Tommy and see what kind of kid he was.

I started dating Tommy that summer. We'd go to the P.S. 60 schoolyard to hang out. Roxanne and Ramona Rizzo and I were the regulars. Jennifer Graziano was joining us, too. She was a girl I had just started hanging out with. She was the daughter of Anthony "The Little Guy" Graziano, an alleged big shot in the Bonanno crime family. She had an older sister, Renee, but Renee ran with a different crowd.

Renee was different from Jenn. She was the true definition of a Mafia princess. She dressed the part with her fur coats and fancy jewelry. I remember sneaking into nightclubs and Renee would be there, hanging out with wiseguys, drinking and having fun. She was the total opposite of Jenn, Ramona, Roxanne, and me. If we went to a club and ran into some of our of fathers' friends, we would run and hide, partly because we were still too young to be out but mostly because we didn't flaunt our dads like Renee did.

Jennifer would sneak out of her house, too, because she was dating a guy named Danny. She lived in another neighborhood off Hylan Boulevard. If we weren't walking to the school-yard, we had other people picking us up. The problem was that when I was dating Tommy, his ex-girlfriend, a girl from my neighborhood, would be hanging around. She was now dating someone else, and her sister and her sister's friends were also dating some of the guys who hung out at the schoolyard of P.S. 60. Tommy's ex hated me because she still had feelings for Tommy. She would call my friends and me names like Mafia princesses or daddies' girls. She was Puerto Rican and knew nothing about the mob. It seemed to me she and her sister didn't get who our fathers were. Whenever this group of girls saw us, they threatened that they were going to kick our asses. One of the guys in the schoolyard warned us that the girls were crazy, the types who would split your face open with a beer bottle or jump you when you were alone. I am not going to lie, I was scared. I knew if I went to my father, he would handle the situa-tion, but going to Dad was not the way I handled my business.

My girls and I started meeting at Roxanne and Romana's parents' house where we practiced fighting each other so we would be ready, just in case they confronted us. Finally, it hap-pened. We wiped their asses and got the respect we deserved. We never used our fathers' names to get the respect. If some-one tried to kick my ass, all I really would have had to have done was to say, "My dad is Sammy." But Dad taught me how to stick up and fight for myself. The first fight we were in was at a nightclub on Staten Island. Back then, you had to be eigh-teen to get into the club, but we had fake ID and would sneak in. I was sixteen. Everybody was on the dance floor. We were battling the girls, bumping each other hard until it turned into an all-out catfight. Even though the place was dark and the music was loud, we had an audience. Luckily, we won.

The one time I got caught sneaking out of the house, I was getting ready to go to a big party. Roxanne, Ramona, and Jennifer were all at my house. They were going to sleep over. Gerard knew I snuck out and he used to help me. He'd go downstairs and turn on the radio and make noise. That night, Gerard decided that he was going to sneak out for the first time. He didn't even need to sneak out. He wanted to see if his minibike, which was in the driveway, had a flat tire, so he could have gone out the front door. My parents were in the kitchen. Gerard didn't have the good sense to walk stealthily. My Dad said to my mother, "Did you hear something?" Mom said no.

Later that night, the four of us used the roof to get out without Dad hearing. We knew how to walk quietly and our escape was successful. But because he'd heard Gerard earlier, he was on high alert. He didn't know we'd snuck out. He never went up to check on us, assuming we were home. So when we were coming back across the roof, making a little noise, he heard something but had no idea it was us.

He ran to get his gun, thinking, "oh my God, here they come, up my kids' window." Footsteps in the night, especially on a roof, meant something else to my father.

He came flying up the stairs, gun in hand. He heard the commotion going on in the bathroom as we tumbled in. Just as he pushed opened the door, I came walking out of the bathroom. We walked right into each other. He had the gun pointed at my head, and I threw my hands up in the air.

"Dad!" I screamed. "We just went to Miggy's to get a sandwich."

"Karen, do you see this?" he puffed, waving the gun.

"Yeah," I said.

He yelled out, "Do you know how close you just came to getting killed?"

"Yes," I answered.

"*Get to bed!*" he directed and slammed the door.

In the morning, my mother came into my room to collect the laundry. Every day, she'd do all the laundry, and everything was ironed and pressed.

"Where's Daddy?" I asked.

"Oh, you're dead," she answered. "When the girls leave, you need to go downstairs and talk to him."

I knew that meant to get the girls out. I was so scared of what he was going to say. I went downstairs and he was sitting at the head of the table, where he always sat. He'd do his books there, always jotting down numbers and crossing them out. This morning, he was stewing, drinking a cup of coffee.

"Do you want to talk to me?" I asked.

"Sit down," he ordered.

Usually, I sat to his right, but I was afraid to be right next to him, so I sat one chair down. He pushed the chair between us out of the way and directed, "Move your chair closer." He continued in a rage, leaning into me. "Do you know how close you came to getting whacked last night?"

"Uh huh."

"Do you know how fucking upset I am right now?"

"Uh huh, I won't do it again."

"I'm not upset that you snuck out of the house. I'm upset that I almost blew your head off your shoulders!"

"I'm sorry."

"You cannot be crawling off my roof at night."

"I'm sorry," I repeated. "I'll never do it again."

"Do you know how serious it can be if I think somebody is sneaking into my house? Do not crawl off my fucking roof again!"

"I'm sorry," I said for the third time, and started to cry.

"Give me a kiss and give me a hug," he said, accepting my apology. "Karen, I swear to God, do you know how sick to my stomach I would be if, God forbid, I would have pulled that trigger?"

"Yes," I replied, promising not to do it again. He made my curfew earlier, which I accepted without protest. That weekend, I snuck out again. Dad was so upset that he had almost killed me, that he never checked up on me again. My father was a man of honor and if he gave you his word, he stuck to it. He expected everyone around him to do the same. Although he knew I was a kid and would probably sneak out again, if he said he was going to trust me, he was not going to run up and check on me every night. If I fucked up and he caught me again, then it would be a big problem. But my father was exceedingly fair and when he accepted my apology, he also gave me back his trust.

Most of the time when I snuck out, I went to find Tommy. Tommy was a decent guy. He got into petty fights and stayed out late, like everybody else I knew. But those weren't crimes. Dad always told me I needed to respect myself as a woman. He wanted me to be with someone who respected me, and he told me he had to meet and approve any guy I dated. I thought I should bring Tommy home, but I was afraid for him. I was daddy's little girl and one thing I knew for sure was if I brought a guy home, he had to be just right. In my experience with him, my father would never hurt somebody, but he was very protective of his family, especially his children.

The grilling started the moment I brought Tommy into the house. Dad started with, "Tommy, you think you can handle going out with my daughter?"

I knew Tommy was already a little intimidated. He was aware my father was the underboss of the Gambino family. I didn't know it, but all the kids in the neighborhood looked up to the gangster life and admired my father, including Tommy.

"You better treat my daughter good," Dad warned.

Tommy and I dated for three years. Eventually, Dad got him a job in construction. If I was gonna be with somebody, he wanted the guy to have a good job and a decent career.

Dad and I became closer during my junior and senior years. We'd work out together at the gym. If I had a couple of pimples, he was the one to run me to a dermatologist. I looked up to him and respected him, not just as a father, but as a friend. I didn't mind being around him. I admired and learned a lot from him, mostly about life. I knew that everything he did was because he loved us. I was the one person in his life who could talk back to him. He'd debate an issue until everyone else gave in, but I would just continue until he gave in. We had a very cool relationship. He loved the fact I never backed down. He liked that I was strong-minded and opinionated. That's why I think he let me get away with winning some of our disagreements. He wanted to see how I handled myself and he liked the fact I was not a pushover. In fact, he encourged me to stand my ground.

He could talk to me about teenage stuff. He warned about drinking and driving. He told me if I was going to a party, and there was going to be alcohol, I should call him if the driver was going to be drinking.

I told him I probably wouldn't call, because I didn't want to get punished for drinking myself. Dad promised me, he'd waive any punishment or reprimand if I called. He knew I was the kind of kid who would still drink but never call if he was going to be angry.

One time, when I was more than a little tipsy, I took his advice and called Mom to come and pick up my friend Valerie and me from a party. Dad thought it was so amusing when he took a look at us coming into the house. "Are they drunk?" he asked my mother. I overheard the question and told him no, we weren't.

"Okay then, let's play craps," he said with a wry smile. He wanted to test me and see if I could handle the dice. I rolled away, but this time I couldn't add up the numbers. Once again, Dad had caught me red-handed. Even though he was a father and would make me answer for what I did wrong, he knew the reality of life and let me be a kid, as long as I didn't get out of hand. He trusted me enough to know that I might not always be perfect, but I was no fool and I knew right from wrong.

When I was seventeen, I returned home from school one afternoon to find my parents in my bedroom. The closet door was open, revealing a typical teenager's disarray. I was about to apologize for the mess when my father suddenly handed me a screwdriver.

"Pop open the third plank," he instructed. There, along the back wall of my closet, was a combination safe. It contained two gold watches and two million dollars in cash.

"It's for an emergency, in case something happens to me or your mother," he said.

That's a lot of money, I thought, staring at the stacks of bills.

I was imagining all the things I could buy at the mall when my father's voice snapped me back to reality.

"And don't let me find out you're going to the mall with this!" he admonished.

Dad always said these real serious things and then lightened them up with a joke.

That year, Gerard broke his leg. He was fourteen, and we had brought his minibike back from my grandmother's house in Pennsylvania. He had been riding it after dark when a car had run into him. The hospital called my dad to tell him there had been an accident, but had no more information. Dad was at Angelo Ruggiero's wake in Howard Beach, Queens. Angelo was a close associate of John Gotti and the nephew of the late Aniello Dellacroce, a Gambino underboss, until he had died of cancer. Just the men went to the funerals. The FBI was always watching the events, so the wives stayed away. My father went to John Gotti and said, "I've got to go. My son was hit on a dirt bike."

John did the sign of the cross and said, "Oh my God, go!" Ruggiero's wake was at the same funeral home where John's son had been laid out. His youngest son, Frank, had darted into the street on his minibike and was hit and killed by a neighbor nine years earlier, when he was only twelve years old. My father's story about Gerard hit John hard.

The guy who had collided with Gerard waited for the ambulance to come. My mother wasn't home. She was at a comedy club in Brooklyn with Huck and his wife, Kathy, and some other friends. Somebody called her there. "Is he gonna die?" she asked. She was told his injuries were not life threatening, but he might have broken his back. My uncle Eddie came over and rode with Gerard to the hospital, and I followed in my own car. I was so scared because I didn't know the extent of the injuries.

Dad found me outside the emergency room at Staten Island Hospital, waiting there for him to come. He jumped out of the car when he saw me, and a cop stopped him on the sidewalk. I thought the cop was going to tell him what happened. He asked my father, "Is this your bike?" When my father saw the minibike, he thought Gerard must be dead. Instead, the cop said, "We'll have to give you a couple of tickets. The bike's not registered."

That set my father off. "You fucking cocksucker, motherfucker. . . ." At that very moment, his jaw got all tight, like it did when he got really mad. "Take the tickets and stick 'em up your fucking ass."

He grabbed me by the arm. "Where's your brother?" he screamed and pulled me into the ER.

"He's fine," I told him, trying to calm him down. "But I think he broke his leg."

"Where were you?" he asked. "You were supposed to be home watching him."

It didn't take long for the hospital lobby to fill up with fifteen guys in suits. John had sent down a couple of guys to make sure Gerard was okay, and everybody else had followed straight from the funeral to make sure everything was under control. They completely took over the lobby. They all brought food and bagels and stuff, a big Italian spread.

The next morning, the driver of the car sent flowers to Gerard's hospital room. Dad and I were there when they arrived. "This is from the guy who hit you," Dad told Gerard. "Do you know how dangerous it is, driving a bike at night? This poor guy, he's freaking out. He wants to leave town. It's dangerous to be riding a minibike at night. You shouldn't be sneaking out."

"And you," he said, turning to me. "You were supposed to be watching your brother."

Later that day, Gerard was back from surgery; a metal rod was put in his leg. The guy who had hit him came by. He apologized, saying it had been an accident. It was at night, and he hadn't seen my brother when he was turning into his driveway. He was still devastated.

I remember seeing how stricken with fear this guy was of my father. It looked like he wanted to take off running and get out of town. I felt so sorry for him because it was not his fault. Everybody knew what happened to the guy who had hit Frank Gotti. He wound up dead, shot execution style with his body put in an acid bath. My dad reassured the poor guy that everything was okay. He sent him away, saying, "Don't worry about it." He even sent him a nice basket of fruit.

PART II

CHAPTER NINE

"Gangsters, they sent flowers for everything."

The road I traveled sometimes did not seem like it was my own. My parents never talked to me about life after high school. There was talk of college, but Dad knew that school was never my strong point. My father had certainly given up on me being a lawyer. I was a fast learner but I was no A student. The problem was, I wasn't really fond of classes and formal education. Dad was gonna help me launch some sort of business instead. Whatever I wanted to do in life, he'd be right by my side helping me.

When I was eighteen and had graduated from Richmondtown Prep, my father asked me "What are we going to do with you, Karen? What do you want to do with your life?"

I said, "A flower shop is a good business." What with all the funerals, weddings, and parties that my friends and their families had to deal with, a florist fit right into the whole scheme of things. So, for my graduation present, my father gave me the keys to my very own flower shop.

It was right next door to his construction headquarters on Stillwell Avenue in Brooklyn. I guess it was part of his master plan for me, that I run my own business. My parents assumed I would run the flower shop, meet a nice guy, get married, and have a family. They wanted nothing but the best for me. Even if it seemed like Dad was trying to mold my life by being so involved, I knew he only wanted me to be on a different path than he was, away from the ups and down that went with the lifestyle he had chosen. He never wanted to worry about Gerard and me or to get the phone call that one of us was in jail. He thrust me into my post–high school life with my best foot forward. His idea of a little flower shop couldn't have been a better plan.

In many ways, the last thing I wanted was the responsibility of running my own business. But if I was going to be in charge, at the very least, I wanted to pick the name of the place. After thinking about it long and hard, I decided to call it Exotic Touch, a name both elegant and tropical. I was very proud of my shop, and it was important to my father. The name Exotic Touch reflected that perfectly.

My father's big thing with Gerard and me was that we should always be responsible, and I'm certain he put the shop next to his headquarters so he could make sure I was taking care of business. He didn't get me the shop just so I'd have something to do. He wanted me to run it, to take it seriously, to be on time. He told me, "Never forget, this place is yours. You're the one who's going to put the key in the door at eight A.M. You should be proud of it."

I was proud of the place, but I was also a kid. The truth was

I didn't know anything about flowers, boutonnieres, bridal bouquets, or centerpiece arrangements. Still, everybody in the entire neighborhood bought their flowers from me, including John Gotti himself, and my business was booming. Catering halls, funeral parlors, and small businesses all placed their orders with me. It seemed like I could charge whatever I wanted, that price was no object. Many of the big bouquets and arrangements were selling for $500 a pop.

I worked grueling hours in the flower shop, opening at eight A.M. and often staying until nine or ten at night to fill all the orders. Gangsters, they sent flowers for everything. We got all the work for the Scarpaci Funeral Home on Eighty-sixth Street, and were the house florist for two local catering halls. Everybody wanted to use us. We were overwhelmed with orders and could barely handle all the work. I was utterly exhausted. Then one day, it suddenly hit me that the reason I was getting so much business was because I was Sammy the Bull's daughter. People respected my father so much they would not take their business anywhere else.

Dad was a feared man, but he was also liked and respected. He always treated the people around him well, helping them to make money. If anyone close to him opened a new business he would be the first to support him, and he expected everyone he knew to do the same. So, when it came time for me to open the shop, everyone he had once helped returned the favor. We were pretty much the florist for the entire Gambino crime family. That was good enough for me. I liked that my store was popular.

In light of my steady stream of customers, Dad brought in a partner for me, a friend of a friend of a friend named Mario. Poor Mario! He was completely stressed out most of the time, knowing he was creating flower arrangements for the likes of John Gotti and Sammy the Bull. The reality was they probably would never have known if the flower arrangments weren't perfect and I am sure they would not have put up a big beef if they weren't one hundred percent satisfied. But Mario was always striving to make sure that all of our arrangements were flawless, just in case. He put a lot of pressure on himself.

John would call us all the time to send out flower arrangements, and every time he did Mario would put himself in a frenzy trying to make them perfect. Plus he had to deal with me, a nineteen-year-old, not-a-care-in-the-world Italian girl who was only casually interested in being a businesswoman, although I was doing my best not to shirk my responsibilities.

After the shop closed, I'd go into the city to party with my friends at the nightclubs. I'd get home at four A.M. and be at the shop at eight with a horrible hangover. Mario would be so paranoid! There would be a funeral or something equally important, and there I was staggering around nauseous from the sweetness of the flowers. Even though I was a kid, and a little on the wild side, I knew how important it was to my father that I be responsible, so I'd work despite the hangovers. I was a lot like my dad. When I did something I gave it my all. At the flower shop, I strove to make him proud.

The funeral pieces were a nightmare for me. I had to cut all the flowers on an angle so they'd be the right height for the arrangement, something that was always huge and elaborate. We'd haul the monster floral pieces to Scarpaci's or the church or both, and then race back several hours later to collect them, bring them back to the Exotic Touch, pull out stems we could use again, and recycle them into something bridal. Mario was taking on most of the stress of the place. I'd be saying, "Don't worry," and he'd be hustling around like a man with a gun pointed at his head. My father never put us under pressure, but I guess he felt it on his own. He acted as thought every order we filled had to be flawless, and if something went wrong, it would all fall on him, even though that was not the case. My father was harder on me. I think he realized the importance of grooming me early so I could be successful. Although I was never good with school, I had definitely demonstrated that I was good with business. I had a certain hustle, a lot like him. I felt that one of my father's main reasons for opening the flower shop was to teach me responsibility and how to run a business; the fact that it was a good money maker was an added bonus. Still, I think I drove Mario nuts.

I had heard that I wouldn't need to charge sales tax for people who chose to pay in cash. The next day, a customer called the shop with a fairly big order, and asked if she could pay with a credit card. I responded, "Sure, but if you pay in cash instead of credit, we won't charge you tax."

Right then, Uncle Eddie wandered into the shop. Being next door at the construction office, he came by once in a while to check in on me for Dad. When he heard what I said, he pulled the phone out of my hand, slammed it down, and yelled, "What're you doing?! There might be a wiretap. You can't say things like that on the phone!"

Dad showed up later that afternoon. Uncle Eddie had clearly filled him in, because the first thing he said to me, before he even said hello, was "Karen, people have to pay taxes. People *want* to pay taxes. You can't tell them something like 'don't pay your taxes' on the phone."

I knew that people didn't really *want* to pay taxes, but I understood my father's hint—don't say that on the phone.

I had owned the shop for less than one year when I started noticing surveillance vehicles watching our building. I had noticed them on a side street near our house as well. I used to see them from time to time when I was still sneaking out of the house. They even knew me by name. One time, I was tiptoeing through the side gate, and one of the agents rolled down his window and said with a smile, "Going out again, Karen?"

Now surveillance had picked up dramatically. It seemed like they were watching Dad twenty-four hours a day.

I understood that John Gotti and my father were running a criminal enterprise, but it was hard for me to envision the illegal part of the business. My father took his work with the construction company very seriously. He followed a very strict regimen. First, he'd start with his workout at the gym in Brooklyn, not too far from the office. Then he'd head for Stillwell Avenue, arriving before noon. He'd stay there until four-thirty or five, making sure he'd be home for dinner at five-thirty. He loved construction and took great pride in it. Although he got most of his contracts because of who he was and his reputation as a feared gangster, he still treated each job with integrity.

With my flower shop right next door to Dad's headquarters, I'd see him sitting behind his desk talking about construction and cement to customers. People would show up at his office, and after they shook hands, they'd do the rest of their business walking along the sidewalk outside my shop. I thought it was a little odd, but I realized later that the only way he could keep his conversations from being recorded was to have them away from the office. Dad would always wave to me when they passed.

I knew they were talking about illegal stuff. And they were being extremely cautious about not being recorded. Although I knew there were illegal activities going on behind the scene, looking at it from my perspective it was hard to envision the criminal side of it because everything appeared on the up-and-up. In the mornings, I would see all the crews climbing onto the Marathon Concrete Corp. trucks and going out. They were dressed in their Marathon construction uniforms, black shirts with red lettering, that Dad had made for all his workers. Friends of the family had them, too. Even Gerard and I had our very own Marathon Construction bomber jackets. Dad's secretary, Sherry, was always at the reception desk, answering the phones, paying the bills, and doing the books. I guess I just really didn't see the criminal side of it. Even though I knew it was there, it didn't matter to me because I saw a man who took pride in what he did. As much as he took pride in being a gangster, that was the side of him he kept hidden as much as possible from his family. The way he ran his business was so organized, I guess that's why they called it organized crime. Dad was so successful in the construction business that he controlled most of the unions in the five boroughs. I think even the people who weren't in the mob didn't mind working with him. A big part of his success was that he made sure the jobs got done.

John Gotti was Dad's "boss," and my father always made sure that John got a large kickback from all the construction jobs he was doing. That's how it worked in the mob. But Dad was pretty much the go-to guy in construction for the Gambino family. Not only did he have Marathon, but he also had his hand in drywall, Sheetrock, excavation, and plumbing companies, to name a few.

"If Donald Trump wants to build a building, he can't do it without us," Dad told me. "We control the unions, so we just call and tell them to stop the trucks."

It was October of 1990 when my father sat the family down and told us he was going on the lam. We had just gotten home from the reception for my cousin Gina's Communion when he summoned my brother and me to his bedroom. I already knew something big was going to happen. The FBI had been staked out in front of my flower shop for weeks. They even had agents in unmarked cars posted outside the reception hall that night. Over the years, I had always been aware of the Feds and their surveillance vehicles, but within the last couple of weeks they were everywhere my father went. By now, I was one hundred percent aware that Dad was the underboss of the Gambino family and for the first time, I felt his world closing in on all of us. It was at this point that I realized that no matter how much he tried to keep us away from it, this was my world as well. Yet I still knew so little about it.

Dad said he was going into hiding from the Feds but he didn't explain why. It was only later that I learned he was running on the advice of John Gotti.

Gotti had learned there was an indictment coming down against him, my father, and Frank Locascio. The three men were going to be arrested and charged with five counts of murder: Paul Castellano; Thomas Bilotti, Paul's underboss, who had been executed with Paul outside of Sparks Steak House; Robert "DB" DiBernardo, a caporegime in the Gambino family, who had been shot twice in the head in 1986; Liborio Milito, a Gambino soldier, who had disappeared in 1988 and whose body had never been found; and Louie DiBono, another Gambino soldier, who was shot and killed in the parking lot of the World Trade Center in 1990 because he didn't obey an order to go and see John Gotti. In addition to the murder charges, Gotti was also facing an indictment on racketeering.

Bugs had been planted by the FBI in a room above the Ravenite Social Club on Mulberry Street and conversations between John and Frankie DeCicco had been recorded, linking my father, John, and Frankie to the murders. Gotti felt they could stall the arrest if my father went away.

Mom was already in the bedroom when Gerard and I came in. He didn't tell us why he was running. I guess he figured the less we knew, the better it would be. "You may read some things in the newspaper, but I just need you to trust me. I'll be okay." We didn't ask any questions and went upstairs to bed. A couple of hours later, Dad came into my bedroom to give me a kiss. "I want you to know I love you," he whispered. "If you need anything, Uncle Eddie and 'Big Louie' and them will be here to take care of you." Big Louie was Dad's friend Louie Valario.

I asked my father when he was coming back. He stopped, stared at me for a bit and said, "I don't know."

When I was a kid, my father would say, "Make a fist." Then, he would make us punch his hand. He would say, "See? When you make a fist and hold your hand tight, it will make you strong. This is like our family. If we always stick and stay tight like a fist, we will always be strong, and nothing can come between us."

No matter what, whether I was playing sports or receiving an award, sick or hurt, it was his way of letting me know he supported me and to stay strong. He had my back, we were one. This signal between us was his way of saying to me everything would be okay without saying it.

I couldn't sleep that night, wondering where he was going. When I got up in the morning, he was gone. For a month, I didn't see him or talk to him. He didn't call. My mother didn't talk about it, but I could tell she felt empty. I'd come home every day, and look in his room to see if he was there. He wasn't, and I felt empty like my mother. I wondered if it was going to be like that for the rest of my life. Not knowing what was going on was worse than anything. Then, speculation came out in the newspapers that Sammy the Bull could be dead.

I went straight to my mother. "Mom, is it true?" I asked her. "Is Daddy dead?"

"No, he's okay," she assured me.

"Did you talk to him?"

"Yes," my mother answered. She hadn't really spoken to him. But someone had gotten a message through.

"Is he ever going to come home?"

"I don't know," she replied.

"I don't understand," I said. "Is this it? Is this how it's gonna end?"

"I don't know how to make you understand, because I don't fully understand," Mom said. In reality, she did understand. She had spent her whole life trying to shield us from Dad's world. She always knew she couldn't keep the reality of Cosa Nostra a secret from us forever. We always had money, food on the table, nice vacations, and a summer house. Dad always made sure Mom drove a nice car. We didn't want for anything. But Mom always realized that one day we would have to face the consequences of the way Dad earned his money. Now, that time was finally here. She accepted that, but she didn't know how to convey it to her children. I had never thought about the death part of it. It was more that when there was a death, everything happening around us seemed bigger than the death itself. I have been dealing with death my whole life, from my uncle Nicky and Stymie on. From the time I was a little kid, my father was going to funerals.

There was a thin veneer disguising all the things my father did. Dad was like Superman. At home he was a mild-mannered father, funny, charming, warm, the soft disciplinarian. When we went out, he had his "Superman" suit. He was elegant, he stood up straighter, and he had an air of authority. I thought he commanded a gentleman's respect, but I found out people were truly afraid of him. He was scary and powerful. He controlled something, although I wasn't sure exactly what. I never saw the other side of Sammy the Bull, the violent, cold executioner side.

Mom had heard of a few men who had gone on the lam before. If they came home at all, they usually went to prison when they got back. There had also been cases of men who had left, changed their identity, and never returned. Others had turned up dead. Because of the risk to the family, when a man went on the lam, he would cut off all ties to his prior life for everybody's safety. My mother was a true mob wife, she never asked questions and she did what she was told. I think she felt that if she ignored things, they would just go away.

This time, I think she realized it was not going away. But she was still unsure how to deal with it. Her motherly instinct kicked in, and she needed to figure out how to protect Gerard and me from what was about to happen.

The morning after the story about Dad possibly being dead appeared in the paper, I awoke to my mother calling to me from downstairs: "Karen, come down here." I went down to the kitchen and Dad was standing there with a full beard and wearing a green shirt. I just started crying. "I thought I was never going to see you again," I said.

"I couldn't stay away, even if coming back means I will have to spend the rest of my life in prison."

"What do you mean?" I asked. "Prison?"

He didn't directly answer the question. We all sat down for breakfast, then Dad went to his bedroom to shave. I never knew where he had been. I wanted to know, but I realized it wasn't the time to get into it. For the first time in my life, I felt like it wasn't my business to ask. At that point, my prison question didn't matter anymore. I was just so happy to have him home, even though my happiness was short-lived.

I later found out that John had thought if my father left town, the Feds couldn't bring the indictments against any of them. The plan was for him to make his way to Brazil and run the family from there. He had been in and around Atlantic City. He was getting passports made up, so he sized up other cities in South America that might make a good base of operation. My father had been under the eye of the FBI even since Paul's death and our move to Lamberts Lane. The whole surveillance thing felt like a game. Dad and his crew would joke about the Feds. From the flower shop, I'd hear Big Louie's big voice saying, "Guys, should we send them some pizza?"

My father wasn't home for long, less than twenty-four hours, when he was summoned by John Gotti to make an appearance at the Ravenite Social Club. Dad was irritated that John wanted to meet at such an obvious place. He would have preferred to meet in a secret location, considering he had a tip from a cop that he and Gotti were going to be arrested, which was why he had gone on the lam in the first place. The Feds had been looking for him day and night for the last month. The surveillance had become so heavy that agents had actually been following Mom and me, thinking we might be meeting him secretly. Although Dad knew that he was coming home to be arrested, he had wanted an extra few days to tie up some loose ends and spend time with his family.

Because Dad was so loyal to John, he agreed to meet him on his terms. When my father left the house that day, he was dressed in jeans, a white T-shirt, a black leather jacket, and socks and sneakers. Normally, when he went to meet John Gotti, he would wear a suit. But he was pretty sure he was going to be arrested that night and had dressed for the occasion.

When he walked out the door that evening, I knew in my heart he wasn't going to come home. I wanted to cry, but I didn't. I looked over at Mom and wondered if she felt the same way I did. It was hard to tell, because she was being strong. It was like we were all going through the motions. It was part of the lifestyle and it came with the territory.

Gerard was upstairs when Dad left. I didn't bother to go in and check on him. But I was sure he was feeling the same way. He was younger than me, and it was almost like we looked at Dad's life through two different sets of eyes. He was a lot like Mom, if he ignored it, maybe it didn't happen. He also may not have been as intrigued by my father's lifestyle as I was.

Dad and I were very close. By nature, I was extremely curious and I liked to know what was going on, especially when it came to my father. I knew that night was different. Everybody assumed Dad was going to be arrested, but nobody was saying it, at least not to me.

Sometimes when Dad would make jokes, I knew he was

making light of a situation. However, he took his role at being a gangster very seriously, with all its pros and cons.

Dad and some of the old-time gangsters didn't like how John handled his business so publicly and predictably. Here they were with all this heat coming down and my father would have to go to the same place at the same time every night, Mulberry Street at six o'clock, to meet his boss. My father always felt that John was giving the Feds the entire Gambino family on a silver platter. The mob was supposed to be a secret society, and by holding their meetings so out in the open, the clandestine element was gone. The old-timers would tell my father to talk to John, to take it down a notch. But John's motto was "Let's put it in their face, let's show them who we are." I guess in his mind, he felt like he was untouchable. But his arrogance made surveillance easy. So the Feds watched and built their case.

When Dad got to the Ravenite Social Club that night John was already there. The club was filled with the Gambino captains and lieutenants who had to report there on a nightly basis to turn in money and discuss the daily operations. My father joined John and Frankie at John's table in the back. They were there only fifteen minutes when the Feds knocked on the steel door with a speakeasy peephole. Dad later told me that John was very calm when the agents came inside.

"We have been expecting you," he said. "We are just going to have our last cup of coffee before we go anywhere." John, my father, and Frankie remained at the back table, sipping on espresso while the agents asked each man in the club to produce his ID and state his name. The men were excused one by one, until only Dad, John, and Frankie were left. The men finished their coffee, heard their Miranda rights, and waited to be handcuffed before they were taken to unmarked cars waiting on Mulberry Street. The three men were driven to the Metropolitan Correctional Center (MCC) in separate vehicles. Somehow the press knew about it, so throngs of reporters were waiting for them to get out of their cars in front of the jail on Centre Street. John was dressed up in his dark pinstriped suit; red, gold, and black necktie; and yellow silk scarf, always polished and ready for the cameras. Dad, meanwhile, answered a reporter who was pointing at him and asking, "Is he one of the guys?"

"No, I got these two guys under arrest," he joked, motioning to the Feds on either side of him. "Everything's under control."

Once inside the MCC, the men were ordered to surrender their street clothes, everything but their socks. Back at the Ravenite before the arrest, John had commented about how Dad had not dressed for the "occasion," meaning the arrest, which would turn into a photo op for John. But now that the men were in jail and stripped of everything but their socks, John didn't seem to mind so much that my dad was wearing thick sweat socks. They were good inside the cold jail. John asked my father if he could borrow them. Dad, ever loyal, took them off and handed them over.

I knew Dad was a gangster, but I thought the news and newspapers were exaggerating what a mobster was. But with my father's arrest, I soon learned that *I* may have been underplaying what it meant to be a gangster. After Dad was arrested, I thought he would be released on bail and be back home with us. We certainly had enough cash to post bail. But that wasn't the way it worked out. John, Frankie, and my father were considered dangerous and a threat to society and were held without any bail.

Left: Debra and Sammy Gravano at their wedding on April 16, 1971. *(Courtesy: Sandra Scibetta)*

Below: Sammy, Karen, and her grandfather, John Scibetta, celebrating Karen's confirmation in the back yard of the house on Legget Place. *(Courtesy: Debra Gravano)*

Left: Exotic Touch Flower Shop. The business was a high school graduation gift to Karen from Sammy. *(Courtesy: Karen Gravano)*

Below: Grand opening party inside Exotic Touch Flower Shop. *(Courtesy: Karen Gravano)*

Right: Debra and Sammy Gravano going to John Gotti Jr.'s wedding. *(Courtesy: Karen Gravano)*

Below: Sammy driving a boat on vacation in Florida, 1986. *(Courtesy: Karen Gravano)*

Above: John Gotti and Sammy Gravano enter the Brooklyn Courthouse in May 1986. *(Courtesy: Yvonne Hemsey via Getty Images)*

Below left: The day Sammy came home after spending a month on the lam, the day before getting arrested with John Gotti in December 1990. *(Courtesy: Debra Gravano)*

Below right: Sammy in Arizona right after he signed himself out of the witness protection program in 1996. *(Courtesy: Debra Gravano)*

Above: Karen with Dave and their daughter Karina at Karen's mom's house in 1999. *(Courtesy: Debra Gravano)*

Below: Gerard, Sammy, and Gerard's son Nick in Arizona in the summer of 1999, a couple of months before the family was arrested. *(Courtesy: Karen Gravano)*

Above: A night out drinking champagne with the old crew in 1997. LEFT TO RIGHT: Drita, Roxanne, Karen, and Maria. *(Courtesy: Jennifer Graziano)*

Below: The old crew reunited for a friend's wedding in September 2011. LEFT TO RIGHT: Jennifer, Ramona, and Karen.

Above: Karen and her daughter Karina at their house in Arizona on the day Karen left to film the first season of *Mob Wives*, August 2011. *(Courtesy: Karen Gravano)*

Left: Karen on the set of *Mob Wives* in September 2011. *(Courtesy: Karen Gravano)*

Following page: A drawing of Al Capone that Sammy completed while incarcerated. *(Courtesy: Salvatore Gravano)*

CHAPTER TEN

"You're the underboss of the most powerful crime
family in the world."

I never got dressed up to visit Dad in jail. There wasn't any reason to. I wasn't there to impress anyone. There were only two rules: *Don't wear anything revealing,* and *don't wear orange,* the color of prison jumpsuits. I never showed much skin, and orange wasn't a particularly good color for me, so that wasn't a problem. All I'd do was blow-dry my hair straight and spike it up on top, the standard "Guidette" look of the day. Then I'd throw on some Cavaricci jeans and a baggy sweater. As long as my collarbone was covered, everything was okay.

The Metropolitan Correctional Center, where Dad was being held, was located in lower Manhattan, right by City Hall, just south of Little Italy. It was kind of ironic to me. When I was a kid, I used to think the cops were the bad guys, not my father.

The jail was a tall brick building with tiny, skinny windows, so tiny and skinny that I always wondered if the inmates could even see anything out of them. I liked to think they could, because that meant Dad could watch us when we walked back to the car after our visits. John, Frankie, and Dad had been sent there on December 11, 1990. All of them had been charged with multiple counts of murder and racketeering. John and Dad were bunked together in a special wing for high-profile inmates. Frankie was in the same area, but he was in a different cell. Visiting from Staten Island was fairly routine for Mom and me. We went at least once a week.

My mother was always an obsessively punctual woman, so the days we went to see Dad, she'd insist we leave our house at least two hours before our scheduled visiting time. The visitors were brought in in groups, so if you were late, you might get shoved back two or three groups, which meant another thirty, sixty, or even ninety minutes of standing around the waiting area.

After we filled out all the proper paperwork, a guard would walk us through a metal detector, then herd us over to a holding area that looked like a small auditorium. There were ten rows of chairs, six seats across. The walls were institutional white. The entire prison felt like a hospital, eerily quiet and antiseptic.

Each group of visitors was allotted a half hour to visit their loved one or not-so-loved one. Even though Dad was thrilled when we showed up right at our appointed time, our punctuality caused him problems with John Gotti. John's own visitors, usually his son John Jr. and his brother, Pete, often ran late. He'd complain to Sammy, "It makes me look like a jerkoff that your family's here first, and my family's not even here at all. You need to tell them not to get here so early." I suspected it was less about John looking like an idiot, and more about him wanting to monitor what Dad was saying to us. John liked to be in charge, even in prison.

My father didn't want to hear John complain about the time thing, so one day he said to Mom, "Listen, Deb, I know you're anxious to see me, but from now on, please wait for John Jr. and Pete to be ready, and you guys can all come up together." Pete, too, was giving Mom shit. He'd say, "Debbie, please wait for us, because when we're not there on time, John'll yell, '*Why're you guys late? They're on time. Why can't you be on time?*' "

John was very meticulous about the way things were done. When someone walked into a room, that person was expected to shake hands with everybody in a certain order. John was first, Dad was second, and so on down the line of command. So in John's eyes, it was very important for him to be pulled out of his cell at the same time as my father. I never figured out why, it was just the way he wanted it done.

Dad and John each had a cell in a wing on the south side of the ninth floor, aptly called 9-s. We never saw the cells; they were off limits. We always met the prisoners in the visiting room, a room that was about the size of an elementary school classroom. There were no tables, only chairs set flush against the walls. The inmates were brought in six at a time, and each prisoner was allowed a maximum of three visitors, so there could be as many as twenty-four people in that small room at a time.

The front wall of the room was clear glass, and there was always a guard or two keeping a close eye on things, or at least on *most* things. From the moment my father and John arrived at 9-s, the guards were in awe of them, *Oh my God, it's Sammy the Bull and John Gotti!* So, during our visits, they'd usually look the other way. The guards weren't the only ones who were impressed. Other prisoners and their visitors wanted to meet the Bull and the Teflon Don, too. They were stars, especially in New York, where people loved hearing about the Mafia lifestyle. If you were a gangster, you were a celebrity, and Dad and John were on top. Other inmates' visitors would give them snacks, chips, or a candy bar from the vending machine. More than once, I saw fellow inmates introduce their visitors to the two of them.

It always amazed me to see the level of respect these men got. In my eyes, even though they were charged with horrible crimes, they still must have been good people because they were so respected by everybody, by men and women, older people, and kids. Although my father and John were being accused of murder, it was hard for me to see them in that light. I loved Dad, and John had always been nice and respectful to me. He seemed like a good family man. He was always sending flowers to friends and family, and people that he cared about.

My father was more than just a father to me. He was my friend and my protector. It was hard for me to see the other side of him, especially with so many people treating Dad and John the way they did.

During our visits at MCC, we weren't allowed to move the chairs, so we'd have to stare at whatever family was seated directly across from us, and the visitors sitting nearby could undoubtedly hear almost everything we were saying. Naturally that meant we could also hear almost anything everybody else was saying, too, but I didn't want to listen to their conversations. We only had a half hour, and I wanted to focus strictly on my dad, so I always ignored them. Everybody kind of made it a point to ignore other people's business, anyway. There were different codes of conduct that applied here, and respecting other people's privacy was an important one. I remember one time, seeing an inmate and his visitor slip into a bathroom together. My father must have noticed me watching, and leaned over and told me to mind my own business. Prison was a whole different world, and you learned very quickly to only pay attention to your own people, the relative or friend in front of you.

Mom was always physically affectionate with my father during visits, more so than she usually was at home. While we were there, she'd often rub his leg or hold his hand. This hadn't happened much when Dad was a free man. Mom liked to rub Dad's head when they were laying on the sofa in the living room, but that was about as touchy-feely as she generally got. But when he was in prison, she missed him and just liked being close to him. When her affection became too noticeable, Dad would say, "Don't do that in here." It wasn't that Dad minded the physical contact, it was that John didn't like it. "Why are you having your wife rubbing your hand?" John asked my father one time. "You're the underboss of the most powerful crime family in the world. It shows weakness."

Dad and John were only allowed three visitors at a time. There would be special days for family visits, and other days when just the men from Dad and John's life would visit them. On family days, John's wife, Victoria, his son Pete, or his daughters, Victoria and Angel, would take turns visiting him. Victoria was a few years older than me, and one time her dad told me that she wanted to be a fashion designer. She always looked well groomed and put together. But I thought she had a certain arrogance to her, just like her dad. She and I would exchange a cordial hello while we waited to see our fathers, but nothing more than that. Mom, Gerard, Aunt Diane, Dad's sister Fran, and my cousin Rena all took turns visiting with Dad on family day.

My father handled his prison situation well. A man who was locked up with him told me, "When your father and John came in, all the guys thought they would be these hard-ass big shots. But here comes your father, boxing in the gym, working out." My father was just like everyone else. He had a way of adapting to whatever environment he was in. That guy knew that my father was someone to be reckoned with, but he could also see that he was fair-minded. People knew how tough he was, so he didn't need to flaunt it.

"He never tried to play up that he was the underboss," the inmate told me. I wasn't surprised to hear that. He had never played it up outside jail, either.

John seemed irritated by the ease with which Dad was able to interact with the other inmates. He was particularly bothered that my father enjoyed his time in the jail gym with the other guys. John once told Sammy, "How do you think this is going to look to the other families? What if you get punched in the face? What if somebody hurts you? It's going to show weakness." To John, there was nothing worse than showing weakness.

Dad replied, "Well, that's what happens when you box, you get hit in the face. You sometimes get banged up."

John wanted Dad to conduct himself more like a boss. He felt that he should be in his cell and be catered to as the Number Two man in the Gambino family. But Dad was never the type to have someone else do his laundry. He preferred to take care of his business for himself. Even out on the streets, Dad seemed to have no problem interacting with top men in other families. My father was a natural-born leader, but he also gained his respect and trust because of his long-standing reputation of being both fair and loyal. But instead of John looking at Dad's social ease and undying loyalty to the people that he cared about as an asset, he viewed it as a threat and resented my father for the good reputation he had built for himself.

To get John off his back, Dad agreed with him. "Yeah, yeah, you're right John," he'd say, but I knew he thought John was nuts.

John was a tough, hard man, but that didn't mean he was all bad. His biggest problem was arrogance. I think a lot of the publicity he got went to his head. He was very cordial to me, though, always ready with a "Hey Karen, how's it goin'?" He also tried to watch out for me in his own way.

During the year that Dad was incarcerated, I got into two car accidents. The first one was near our house in Staten Island. I blew past a stop sign on the top of a hill in my black Nissan Maxima, and a guy T-boned me on the passenger side. My brother broke his collarbone, and the car was totaled. Okay, it wasn't one hundred percent totaled, but we took it to a car pound, or a chop shop, depending on how you look at it, run by one of Dad's friends, who made sure it looked one hundred percent totaled when the insurance people showed up.

After the second crash, which wasn't nearly as bad, John took me aside in the prison and said, "I've gotta talk to you about these car accidents. What's going on here?" I explained, "Well, John, I'm just learning how to drive." I'd been driving since I was twelve, so the "new driver" excuse wasn't entirely true.

He said, "Karen, by the time this is all over, I hope you know how to drive, because God forbid if something happens to your father, I'm not going to be able to afford to take care of you with all those cars you're going through." I laughed and didn't think anything more of it. But my father was really bothered by what he said. Dad was one of those people who analyzed every word. I could see him thinking after John's comment, and I am sure his mind was going over what John could have meant.

Around this time, I started seeing a transformation in Dad's and John's relationship, mostly because of what was going on in their criminal case. Things exploded after a bail hearing on December 21, when some of the secretly recorded conversations between John and Frankie were played in open court.

My father was sitting next to John at the defense table when the tapes were played. The recordings had been made on December 12, 1989, from an FBI bug planted in an apartment above the Ravenite Social Club. The apartment belonged to a widow of a Gambino family member. The bugs got there after the FBI took notice that the men weren't doing their secret business their usual way, walking up and down the sidewalks of Little Italy.

They figured out that they were using the apartment and gained access to the place while the widow was out of town on vacation. Gotti hadn't swept the place for bugs, assuming it was secure.

On the recordings, John basically was bashing my father and acknowledging that Sammy had committed murder. But he lied about why the murders were carried out, claiming that Sammy had bullied him into sanctioning the hits when in fact it was the other way around. He also accused my dad of being greedy and withholding money from his construction businesses, which was also a lie. Dad had given John more than $1.2 million in cash, from just his construction business alone.

Sitting in court that day, my father could barely contain his anger. Not only was he mad for all the lies John was spewing, but he was also furious that John had put the family in the predicament they were in by insisting that their meetings be held in such an location, right over the Ravenite.

My father was smart enough to know that conversations like the ones on the tape meant that John had been laying the groundwork for him to get whacked. Dad was convinced that John's reason for wanting to get rid of him was jealousy. John had always been envious of Dad's standing with the guys on the streets.

The Feds knew that my father had sworn his loyalty to John. They also knew that he wouldn't react well when he heard John dissing him to Frankie on those tapes, which is why they played them for both men at the same time during the court appearance. Then they locked them down together in a holding cell. True to the FBI's plan, the tapes caused a huge rift between John and my father.

Sammy asked John if he had anything to say to him. He was fuming, hot as could be, but I think all he wanted was an apology and he could have been settled down. Not only did John skip the apology, he made it seem like his ranting on the tapes was my father's fault. Dad had made him angry, he said, and he had just been blowing off steam to Frankie on the tapes, not meaning a word he said.

Dad could see he wasn't going to get an apology. If John had meant it or was just venting didn't matter, either way he was now on the hook for murder.

My father wasn't stupid. He smelled that John was up to something, that John was plotting to set my father up for the fall. The only way Dad could fight the case now was to put in for a severance. He'd need his own defense attorney, who would have to show that John had been lying on those tapes. Sammy got a note to John through the lawyer that he wanted to be tried separately and hire his own attorney.

John sent word back to my father, telling him he couldn't do that. "What would my public think?" was John's reply. "Besides, the streets need John Gotti."

My father was even more upset. The Cosa Nostra's strength was that it was a secret society. When the members took their oaths, they vowed to recognize their Mafia family *before* even their own families. They no longer recognized the government's rules and regulations, and they took in very little of the public's opinion of them. Cosa Nostra was their government, and their loyalties were supposed to be to each other. Who the hell cared what the public thought of John? Dad's ass was on the line for murder.

Not only was John refusing to let the men's cases be severed, but he informed my father that he would no longer be allowed to listen to the tapes and said that Dad and Frankie could only meet with the lawyers when Gotti was present. This was John's way of controlling the three men's defenses. I am pretty sure that Frankie was not happy with the way things were going down, either.

My father later told me that Frankie had come to him in jail, suggesting the two should kill John while they were in custody. Dad said he contemplated it, and had even made a list of people he would have to kill next if he decided to murder John. The list included John's brother, Peter, and even his son, Junior. After thinking long and hard, my father decided against the plan and ripped up the list, focusing on his defense. He would deal with John after they were done with their legal issues, whether it be inside the prison or on the streets.

From that point on, I started to see a change in my father. He seemed disheartened. I think this might have been the first time he ever questioned his oath to the Mafia. He had taken an oath to a brotherhood, and he had been betrayed by a brother.

CHAPTER ELEVEN

*"I'm going to do something that goes against everything
I've ever believed in."*

One day in early October of 1991, Dad summoned Mom, Uncle Eddie, and me to the Metropolitan Correctional Center. He told us to make sure we got there early, even earlier than usual. He sounded very tense, which didn't surprise me. Both he and Uncle Eddie had been acting really strange for the previous two weeks, especially when they were discussing the serious charges Dad was facing.

Rain was coming down in buckets that day. I sensed something big was about to happen and that my life was about to change for the worse. Both in person and on the phone, Dad seemed to be tired and disgusted with everything. I was concerned, because he generally had a positive attitude about jail and life on the inside. Since his arrest, he'd always made it clear that he was doing absolutely everything he could to make the best of the situation, like everything was going to be okay. "Stay strong," he'd say. "We'll always be a family, no matter what."

That day, as soon as Dad walked into the visiting room, I knew something was wrong. He wasn't making his grand entrance, all high-fives and hugs. This time, he looked very serious, like something heavy was on his mind.

Mom, Uncle Eddie, and I were the only ones in the room. The rest of the inmates were doing their visiting in an adjacent room out of earshot. Dad sat down in between Mom and me, and Uncle Eddie took a seat to Mom's right.

I could tell Dad had something extremely serious on his mind he wanted to talk to me in particular about. I watched as he took a long, deep breath, looked directly into my eyes and said, "I'm going to do something that goes against everything I've ever believed in, and everything I've ever told you guys to believe in. I'm going to cooperate with the government. I'm going to testify for them."

I was hearing his words, but I couldn't believe he was actually saying them. I jumped out of my seat, "How can you do this?" I yelled.

"Sit down!" Uncle Eddie directed with a stern voice.

I obeyed, but I was in total shock. What Dad was saying meant that he would be fingering friends, family, and people he'd worked with forever. His testimony was going to put people we'd known all our lives into prison for years and years. Yes, I loved him and wanted him out of prison as soon as possible, but turning state's evidence went against every rule of behavior I had ever known, against everything he had ever taught us to believe in.

From the time we were young, my father told Gerard and me,

"You never give anybody up, no matter what." I'd get punished for telling on Gerard, and he'd get punished for telling on me. Once, Gerard and I had a dispute over the thermostat. It controlled the temperature for the upstairs part of our house, and it was located in Gerard's room. Gerard liked the house really cold, so he'd turn down the temperature and blast the air conditioner, then lock his door. He wouldn't open up, no matter how hard I banged. We'd be up there screaming at each other, then I'd go downstairs to tell Dad, and he'd say, "I don't want to hear it. Go back up there and work it out yourselves." He'd intervene if we were really killing each other, but most of the time, we never told on each other, because that wasn't the way it worked. Whether it involved something big or little, you just didn't do it, plain and simple.

When Dad dropped his bomb, I never felt so hurt, confused, mad, or scared in my entire life. The life I thought I had was gone. With that one announcement, he ripped my heart out. As a child, I had been Daddy's little girl. I looked up to him, respected him, and trusted him. Despite his occupation, I always felt safe and completely protected. Now, I felt totally and utterly betrayed. I stood up and yelled right there in the visitor's room, *"How could you do this?!"*

He was sullen and withdrawn when he said in a low voice, "I know this is something you will never understand, but this is something I have to do."

"You're right," I barked back, "I'll never understand. I don't even know who you are." I even challenged him, "So you're gonna become a rat?" In our circle that was just about the worst thing you could be called.

My father didn't say a word. I think it broke his heart to see me react with so much anger. He quietly told me, "I understand how you're feeling. This is something I've thought long and hard about. I just want you to know that I love you and I'll always love you. I'm not doing it because I'm scared of staying in prison. I'm just done. I'm sick of this life. I'm sick of the backstabbing and the double-crossing. But I also know who I am. I never let anyone in my entire life double-cross me and fuck me over without doing something about it. John is a double-crosser, and I am a master double-crosser."

That afternoon, my father, protector, and friend broke my heart. I was completely empty inside. I could barely even look him in the eyes. Right before our tense good-byes, Dad said, "I told the government I needed two weeks to tell my family, then to get my life in order. This will all come out next week."

He forewarned me there were other bombshells to come. "You're going to hear about murders, about everything we never spoke about at home," he said, with a "by the way" tone. With that, our visit was over.

Naturally, the cold rain was still coming down as Mom and I huddled under an umbrella on the way back to the car. Uncle Eddie drove us home to Staten Island, and Mom kept looking back at me and asking, "Are you okay? Are you okay?"

I definitely wasn't okay. While we were crossing the Verrazano Bridge, I stared out at a raindrop that had started making its way down my window. I felt exactly like that, a raindrop in a storm with nowhere to go but down. When I had left the house that morning, I was a certain person. I had a specific identity. I was Karen Gravano, the daughter of the Bull. But now, my entire life had changed and I was going home the daughter of "Sammy the Rat." I was a new person, and I was as lost as if my father had just stolen my soul.

Uncle Eddie dropped us off at the house. As I got out of the car, he said, "You know you're not allowed to say anything to anyone. None of your friends, nobody. If you do, you might get killed to keep your father from talking. Your brother might get killed, too." He probably didn't believe it, but was just trying to scare me. I could tell he was scared, too. He thought *he* was going to get killed. Right before he pulled away, he gave me one last hard look and said, "Karen, do you understand?" I understood all too well.

Uncle Eddie was a good-looking man with silvery-gray hair, and like John Gotti, he was always dressed to the nines: nice suits, nice ties, nice shoes. He was quiet, and not particularly tough or charismatic, especially when compared to Dad. My father was the kind of guy who was always joking around, throwing fake right hooks and left jabs at people. Uncle Eddie, on the other hand, was a bit more sophisticated and reserved, and never a whole lot of fun.

Dad liked him as a brother-in-law, and he respected him for his knowledge in the construction business. But when it came to the mob, Dad wasn't one hundred percent sold on him. When my father brought him into the life, he was looking at it as an opportunity to help Eddie provide for his sister. But there were other parts of the mob he didn't think Eddie was cut out for. Some of the guys in Dad's crew who were very loyal to Sammy didn't trust Eddie, and they had warned my father about him on more than one occasion. But Dad went against his better judgment and their advice and kept Eddie around. No matter what he felt about him, my father's loyalty lay with his sister. He honored his loyalty to his family more than he didn't trust Eddie, so he didn't want to chase him off.

It was actually Uncle Eddie who first talked with my father about cooperating. He had heard from a lawyer that John was planning to set my father up to take the fall. His defense was going to be that he had lost control of Sammy the Bull, and the brunt of everything would be put on my father. John was hoping that a judge and jury would view him as a victim as well; poor John had lost control of his underboss, Sammy the Bull, mad killing machine. He hoped they would show him leniency, and that he would be spared a heavy prison sentence. Dad, on the other hand, the fall guy, would probably go away to prison for the rest of his life.

I think in Uncle Eddie's heart, he thought that Dad would never actually go up against John. But once Eddie planted the seed, and my father thought long and hard about what Gotti was doing, he decided cooperating was his best option.

I can't say that Uncle Eddie's encouragement was the only reason why my father decided to do what he did, because Dad was no pushover. Everything he did, he did only after he thought it through, long and hard. But Uncle Eddie definitely started him thinking. Plus, he gave Dad his assurance that he would be there to take care of Mom, Gerard, and me, probably making it easier for my father to go through with it.

The day Dad told us he was turning, I noticed that Eddie wouldn't look him in the eye. Dad did this symbolic thing where he would clench his hand in a fist as if to say, *Stay strong, we're one.* When Dad raised his fist that day, Uncle Eddie turned away. My father knew right then and there that Eddie had decided to turn his back on him.

What Dad was doing was extremely bold and risky. He was a strong personality with strong convictions. When he put his mind to something, he did it one hundred percent. I don't think Uncle Eddie had quite the same conviction. Although he had been able to talk with Dad about cooperating, Dad going through with it created a whole different set of problems. Not that Eddie would be the one taking the stand against John, but just associating with someone who switched sides would have earned him the same stigma. And Eddie wasn't the one in jail facing a life sentence for murder. He was out on the streets living his life. He had grown sons and daughters, with families and children of their own, so at the last minute, maybe he just felt this wasn't the right move for him.

I didn't know this until much later, but Dad had called my mother soon after we left the correctional center that day. He told her that Uncle Eddie was not on board. Mom confided to him that, sadly, she also could not get behind him. She let him know she had no intention of going into a witness protection program and was against his decision to cooperate. She was going to stay in Staten Island with her children.

Mom told Dad that she would always love him, but she said that she had never been involved in the life, or the decisions he made when it came to Cosa Nostra. She wasn't about to start now. He was on his own.

My father was what some people referred to as a "Shylock's Shylock," which meant he lent money to people, who would then lend it to somebody else, presumably at a higher interest rate. Dad was owed a lot of money on the streets, probably over a million dollars. I was never sure what happened to it, if it was collected by someone, or if the debts were just squashed, but it was never turned over to us. I am sure my father was particularly bothered that Eddie did not help to collect, but now that he made his mind up to cooperate there was no turning back.

Once we got home from the jail, I went up to my room. I had a million things going through my head, most of them not good. Where were we going to live? What was going to happen to us? Who was going to take care of us? The next day, I went to the flower shop. Uncle Eddie was in the construction office, sitting down at Dad's desk. He could see that I was upset.

"Walk with me," he said.

We went for a walk like I used to do all the time with my father, only this time I was talking about my father. At the time, I didn't know that Uncle Eddie had decided not to go along with my father.

"Where are we going to live?" I asked.

"We're staying put for the time being. You, your mother, and Gerard will stay in the house, and I will take care of the business and I will take care of you."

Then, he patted me on the head and said, "Everything's going to be okay."

It was very confusing to me. I felt like I still had so many questions, but I didn't want to ask.

During the next week, business at the flower shop was normal. No one except Uncle Eddie seemed to know anything, and he appeared to be fine. We didn't really talk about Dad's decision at home. One night, Mom took me out to eat at the local diner. She told me that she would always protect Gerard and me. I told her that I would never go into the witness protection program, and she assured me that we would not have to do that. I could see that she was very hurt by my father, and that she was angry. But she didn't bash him or speak badly of him. "We're on our own," she said.

I think we both felt that we wanted no part of Dad's cooperation, although neither one of us was ready to cut him out of our lives completely.

I couldn't understand why Dad was doing what he was doing. I asked my mother if she could explain it, but she didn't really have any answers, either. All she said was that this was probably the hardest thing my father ever had to do in his life. And she knew that he loved us, no matter what.

CHAPTER TWELVE

"You're not going to get shot in the head."

Right before news of Dad's cooperation was made public that November, Dad called my mother. He signed his agreement to testify against John Gotti in exchange for up to twenty years in prison for all previous crimes. He put his own conditions into the agreement, saying he wasn't going to testify against anyone on his own crew. He told my mother he wanted to see us one last time. He had already been moved from the MCC to the Marine base at the FBI's headquarters in Quantico, Virginia, so we would have to travel there.

Later that day, quite out of character, my mother announced she wanted to take my brother and me shopping at the Woodbridge Center Mall in New Jersey. As soon as we stepped out of our car, we were approached by FBI agents who instructed us to get into their black SUV. The agents were the same men

I had seen on television taking my father, John, and Frankie into custody at the Ravenite.

Dad really wanted to speak to us. He wanted to explain his side. And he wanted to make sure we were okay. He wanted to see us one last time.

I couldn't believe it was really happening. My father was going to betray the Godfather. In my heart, Dad had betrayed me, as well. He had broken his word. Here was my father, who'd given me a certain code of honor, albeit a twisted one. But it was all I knew, and he had violated that code. I was fit to be tied. In a few short hours, I would become known to the world as the rat's daughter. At least he had bars to protect him. I was out there, a moving target in a hostile world.

I looked at my mother and defiantly declared, "I am not going."

"Yes, you are," she replied. "If you never want to see your father again after this, you don't have to. Just go this one time, for me."

I don't know why my mother agreed to the meeting. I know she still loved my father and wanted to hear what he had to say. She didn't agree with what he was doing, but she was also confused, scared, and looking to him for answers. In her heart, she knew that my father loved his family more than anything and that no matter what decision he made, he would always guide us in the right way. Mom had never had to make decisions without him before. I wondered if part of her believed that by going to the prison, she could convince him to change his mind. Or maybe she hoped that he would direct her as to how to carry forward when the story hit the news.

The next thing I knew, we were on our way to the airport to catch a chartered plane heading for Quantico.

"You have to be kidding me," I said in a sarcastic tone, as the agents led me onto the five-seater airplane. I was fuming mad and needed to let it out.

"Karen, please don't do this," my mother pleaded.

Gerard, as usual, remained passive, going along with everything. At fifteen, he didn't understand how complex and earth-shattering everything that was about to happen really was. He just wanted to see our father.

"I hope this plane crashes and we all die!" I said during the ninety-minute flight to our destination.

Dad was waiting for us in a hotel room close to the FBI headquarters. He looked good. He was in shape and in strong spirits. I was surprised to see how confident he was.

"How are you doing?" he asked when he saw us, as if nothing at all had changed.

At that moment, I just wanted to be his little girl again. I wanted to throw myself into his arms where I would be safe and protected. I wanted to tell him something new I had learned that day. But I was far too angry for that feeling to last, and I threw myself down in a chair across the table from him. "I'm not going into witness protection!" I objected.

That was my greatest fear, that not only would I be ripped out of my former life but I'd be sent to Nebraska to become a cow herder.

"No one's asking you to go into witness protection," my father assured me.

"I'd rather get shot in the head than go into witness protection," I wailed.

"You're not going to get shot in the head," said Dad, discounting that fear as well.

"How do you know?" I demanded. I wanted my father to stop

this new destiny immediately and was convinced I could persuade him to change his mind. Seeing me so upset would surely convince him. I was hoping that I could have my way if I applied the right amount of childish protest. At that moment, I just wanted my family back. I just wanted my father to come home. I was overcome by a strong feeling of abandonment, even though my father was standing right in front of me.

Dad and I talked for a while. During our meeting, Mom made it clear that we would not join him in witness protection, but she would never do anything to hurt him. She didn't cry that day, but I did.

I had always thought of my father as the decision maker and my mother as the one who went along with him. But today, she was taking a stand for herself. I had never seen her like this before. There was no arguing or fighting, as we all shared our feelings. Mom surprised me when she told Dad how she felt and what she intended to do.

Dad hadn't called us there to persuade us to join his team. He explained why he was cooperating. We told him we understood his position, but we didn't agree with it.

Mom advised him that we would be staying on Staten Island. Dad asked that we keep an open line of communication. He wanted to be able to check in on his kids. We agreed to stay in touch. We had never been a part of his world and we weren't going to start now.

When I walked out of the hotel room that afternoon, I didn't know if I would ever see my father again. Even though I was still angry, I was also ambivalent. But I realized that when people make a decision, it is their decision, and I can't change it. I was heartsick. I just wanted to go home to Staten Island.

By the time we arrived home from Virginia that evening, the story of Dad's cooperation had already hit the airwaves. It was breaking news on the radio and on television. CNN was carrying the story nonstop. News reporters were even breaking into television programs, the story was so big. Reporters were already gathered outside of our house on Lamberts Lane when we pulled up that night. We had an electric garage door, so Mom drove the car straight into the garage, and shut the door behind us.

Not long after we got inside, the doorbell rang. It was Uncle Eddie, "Big Louie," Huck, and some other guys from Dad's crew. Looking at their expressions, I guessed everybody felt the same way I felt, brokenhearted. They had been clueless that Dad was going to turn and were all in shock—except for Uncle Eddie, who was only *pretending* to be in shock.

One by one, they hugged Mom. Uncle Eddie asked my mother for whatever guns or silencers were in the house. She handed them over. She also gave him all of the books and ledgers of all the money that Dad was owed from people on the streets. We did have money stashed away, but no one asked for the money. I guess that wasn't important to the men.

The guys were in the house for a while. Mom made coffee for everyone. I could tell she was nervous. She assured the guys that she didn't approve of Dad's cooperation, and that she had no intention of leaving Staten Island to join him. Big Louie delivered a message from John. He told Mom that John realized that she was a woman and not a gangster, and that she had had nothing to do with my father's decision. He sent his assurance that nothing would ever happen to her or her children.

Uncle Eddie came into the kitchen, sat down at the table

and said, "I can't believe Sammy would do this. Debbie, when he calls, you have to talk him out of it! Tell him to take himself out, to do what he has to do."

While Uncle Eddie was making his rant, I got a drink out of the refrigerator. Big Louie had been watching me and asked if I was okay. I did everything I could to hold back tears. "Yes," I stuttered.

Uncle Eddie pointed at me and said, "How could he do this to you? You tell him he needs to do what he has to do if he calls. He can't go through with this. He has to take himself out."

I was confused by the way Uncle Eddie was acting. I didn't know the extent to which he had agreed to help my father, or if he had at all. But I knew he had been in that meeting with me and Dad at the jail when he first told us about his decision.

Did he really want me to tell Dad to kill himself? "Okay," I said, not sure how to feel. I was scared, angry, confused, hurt, and alone.

Right then, Gerard was walking down the stairs. He took everything in for a few seconds, then turned right around and went back upstairs.

That night, my father called the house collect. He was now back in protective custody at Quantico. He asked me how I was, and I responded in disbelief. "How *am* I? How do you think I am? It's all over the news. They are calling you a rat. Why are you doing this to us? Please don't do this, you can't go through with it." I was crying, and my crying got him choked up. It was the weakest I'd ever heard him sound, but I was really mean in spite of myself. I just couldn't stop assailing him.

He didn't answer my brokenhearted questions, and he asked instead, "Who's at the house right now?"

I answered, "Uncle Eddie and Louie and everyone." Then I passed on Eddie's message.

Dad knew exactly what "do what he has to do" meant. He said, "You're right, I can't go through with this, I can't cooperate. This is not me."

I felt relieved to hear that he couldn't cooperate. But then I realized what that meant. He had gone too far to turn back now. So by him saying I can't go through with it, he meant he was going to kill himself.

I started bawling. I could hear Dad trying to reassure me that it was going to be okay. But I couldn't stop crying. "I don't know who to trust," I wailed. "I don't know what to do." I handed the phone to my mother.

Later, Dad told me that our conversation that night had been one of the most horrible moments of his life. He said he really hit rock bottom. To hear his kid so confused and so hurt by his actions was devastating. He couldn't imagine what I was going through, feeling so scared and unsure of who to trust. I didn't know this then, but my father had told Eddie that if he couldn't go through with his decision, that he wanted him to bring cyanide to the prison so that he could end his life.

Uncle Eddie told us that he was going to give us something to bring to Dad. I didn't ask any questions, but I assumed that it was something for him to use to kill himself. The whole scene was surreal. People he'd known all his life were asking me to help him commit suicide. I was beside myself and I couldn't take it anymore. Bawling my eyes out, I ran up the stairs to my bedroom. I had to escape the kitchen to keep my sanity.

Uncle Eddie followed up the stairs right behind me. He looked me in the eyes, and he said, "I'm your father now, don't ask no questions, and you don't talk about nothing."

"I'm your father now," he repeated. "Your father left you, so I am going to be the one to take care of you and you need to respect me."

"But Uncle Ed . . ." I started without getting very far. I wanted to ask him what was going to happen next.

"But Uncle Ed nothing," he interrupted. "I'm your father now. What I say goes."

About a half hour later when the house was finally empty, I asked my mother why she didn't say anything when everyone was in the kitchen. "Trust me. Your father's not going to take himself out. Don't trust anyone. We're on our own now."

I realized that night that even though my father was really close to these men, they were no longer his family. They had been so loyal to him that he had once considered them brothers. But Dad had switched sides, so those days were over. I was so blown away. I was nineteen and I wasn't a gangster. I didn't understand a gangster's life, even though I was a gangster's daughter. I certainly didn't know what the hell I was going to do next.

That night, for the first time in my life, I understood what Cosa Nostra was really about. It was about choosing *the* family over *our* family, an ancient loyalty to the greater cause.

CHAPTER THIRTEEN

"R.I.P."

That night, I went to bed with nightmares about cyanide. I felt like some of the people who had been friends of the family were now our enemies, but I didn't know which ones were which. I had never had to trust Mom to be the one to keep us safe, and here she was, at the helm for the first time and in god-awful conditions, in the middle of a terrible tempest.

The next morning, I got the shock of my life when I saw the headline in the *New York Post*—R.I.P.—with the names of Dad's nineteen murder victims on tombstones. Sammy the Bull, my father, had killed nineteen people. It was there on the paper's front page that I discovered what my father had really been doing all those years. I had been given little hints throughout my childhood that something was not aboveboard in the Gravano home, and I had spent a good deal of my childhood trying to put the pieces of the puzzle together. Maybe I should have figured it out the first time Dad made the *Post* headlines, but I was only a kid back then.

For hours, I stared at the *Post*'s front page. The article said that the murders had started before I was born. The most recent was only two years earlier. The tombstones all had names on them, some of whom I recognized as onetime family friends, like Louie Milito and Mikey DeBatt.

Louie's daughter, Dina, was a friend of mine. I even remembered when her dad went missing. Dina had come to our house tearfully asking my father to help find him. Dad and Louie had been lifelong friends. Mikey DeBatt was Dad's bouncer at The Plaza Suite, and had been in on the hit on Fiala. My father had always talked highly of Mikey. But his addiction to crack cocaine had made him a liability. The details of Paul Castellano's and Frank Fiala's murders were also in there. Dad hadn't actually pulled the trigger on Fiala, but he had orchestrated the hit and spat on his corpse.

From the article in the *Post,* I learned that Paul Castellano's assassination was a total mob execution arranged by John Gotti, who had feared that Paul was going to kill him because John's crew had been selling drugs behind Paul's back. A four-man hit team, wearing tan trench coats and black Russian hats, had carried out the hit. Castellano was in his car on his way to a dinner meeting at Sparks Steak House. Dad and John Gotti were parked across the street from the restaurant in John's Lincoln, watching out for Paul's arrival. A second hit team was down the sidewalk in case the first four marksmen missed. My dad was another backup shooter, but the execution went down without a hitch, everybody escaped, and John became the boss.

I kept looking at the names on the nineteen tombstones. To my abject horror, one of them carried the name of my mother's brother, Uncle Nicky Scibetta.

For years, I'd thought that my uncle had simply vanished, that he had run away. I later heard that his hand was found, and we all assumed he was dead. Uncle Nicky's death had been the first loss I had ever had to deal with. It still affects me to this day. I had been very close to him. He and I used to go together to the park, and he would take me to Nellie Bly Amusement Park near my grandparents' house in Brooklyn, where we would go on the carousel.

I tried not to think about what could have happened to him. Even after my family held a memorial service for him, I continued to imagine that he would come home to us one day. His death was something that I had always blocked out as too painful to deal with. As a family, we never really talked about Uncle Nicky's passing. Now it was in the newspaper that my father had had a hand in it, and I didn't know how to feel.

At first, I was extremely angry and lashed out at him when he called on the phone. I didn't want to bring it up to my mother. I could see it was something that hurt her deeply also, and she told me she didn't want to talk about it with me, ever. To this day, we have never discussed it. I can't speak for her, but for me, it took a long time. Like my mother, my grandparents also chose not speak about Uncle Nicky. The one thing my grandmother did say was, "The day I learned your father was involved was the day I lost two sons."

I'd never really thought about the murder part before, not even when it came to Uncle Nicky. I did a good job of blocking it out. I may have suspected that murder was a part of my father's life, but I'd never really thought about the men who lost their lives. The way it was portrayed, it seemed like all of the casualties had been involved in this life in one way or another. They knew what they were getting into and that murder was a part of it. Those who were not made men but chose to be around these men, and dared to rob, steal, or violate them, also knew the consequences. These were men who had chosen this life and were fully aware that murder was a part of it. And, in fact, many had committed murder themselves.

A lot of people glamorize this lifestyle, and only choose to look at the glitz and the glory, but the cold reality of this world is murder, and that is not something people think about when they romanticize the Mafia. Looking back, families of the Mafia pay the consequences for actions that we had no part in.

I met the news of my father's defection and his nineteen murders with a mix of horror and fascination. At the time, the news media was playing it out that John Gotti was the good guy and my father was the cold-blooded killer. As odd as this might sound, after I acknowledged the horror of what Dad had done, I found morbid comfort in knowing that he was such a dangerous man, only because I was so scared of what could happen to Mom, Gerard, and me now that my father had switched sides. Even with him in jail, I hoped that people might think twice before they tried to hurt us. There was one thing I was certain about, that he would go to any length to protect me and my brother.

Unlike Victoria Gotti, whose father was still revered despite the fact that he was a mob boss and had also been involved in murder, my family lost every shred of respect we'd ever earned in the Mafia underworld. That's what happened when a person cooperated.

Dad was the enemy because he had cooperated. He was instantly shunned by his community and was morphed and mutated from Sammy the "Bull" to Sammy the "Rat." Experts on the Mafia described my father as the highest-ranking American mobster to break his silence and testify, and to this day, there hasn't been an informant whose impact on organized crime has been so significant. Not even Joe Valachi, a low-ranking member of the Genovese crime family and the first mobster to break the Mafia's code of silence when he testified before a Senate subcommittee in 1963, had had the impact that my father did.

John Gotti was considered the most powerful crime figure since Al Capone, and my father was turning his back on him, on the whole mob, for that matter. In that moment, I lost all of the privileges I'd become accustomed to while growing up. But more important, I started questioning my father's decision, something I never did before in my life. As a child, if my father told me something, I never second-guessed him. I was always content with his answer, but this time, I had a bunch of questions. I started wondering why he was betraying his boss when he had counseled me throughout my lifetime that you never rat out a friend. I was left with all sorts of doubts.

In the hours after news of my father's defection hit the newsstands, my three best friends, Jennifer Graziano and Roxanne and Ramona Rizzo, called me to say they were coming by. They were all daughters of men connected to my father's lifestyle, and we had been lifelong friends. But I was second-guessing everything. I hung up the phone. *Oh my God,* I thought. *Are these girls going to set me up?* Deep in my heart, I knew they would never do that. But I still asked myself that question.

The three pulled up in front of the house but didn't get out of the car. I scoped out the street before stepping away from the front door, and ran out to talk to them.

The girls were hysterical. "We're not allowed to see you any-more," they sobbed. I was completely devastated. What had I done? Why were people in my circle judging me because of who my father was?

Although I felt confused, I was smart enough to know that this is what they had to do. We had all been brought up with the same beliefs. By cooperating, my father was going against everything we had been taught, and I am sure that their fa-thers had wanted them to distance themselves from me, so they didn't have to be involved in the situation in any way. Still, it felt surreal. I never thought that I would be the one in this position.

Our friendship almost mimicked that of our fathers' broth-erhood. We were like a sisterhood. We were like our own "crew." Now, I was forbidden to enter their homes and our sisterhood was being put to the test. "Don't worry, Karen, we're going to figure this out," they promised me. "We love you. We're like sisters." I was so relieved when I realized that they would not abandon me.

Soon after they pulled away, my beeper started going off, and all my other friends were paging me. I couldn't bring my-self to call any of them back. These were friends I'd known my entire life, and I couldn't bear talking with them. All I could think was, *My life's over. I'm only nineteen, and my life is done.*

I didn't realize it at the time, but I, too, was in jail, only I was on the outside, not locked away. It felt like my father had torn me out of my world. At nineteen, I no longer had my fa-ther around, and I didn't know what would happen from one moment to the next. Would my family and friends shun me permanently? I felt angry, abandoned, and alone. But I knew that my father still had people who respected him and would look out for us. Some of the men may have understood why my father cooperated, although they would never say it out loud. Still, they would watch out for me, Mom, and Gerard. Besides, there was that old rule that wives and children were "off-limits."

The flower shop my father had given me for my high school graduation present had been a hot spot of activity from the day it opened right up to the day his defection became front-page news. Overnight, customers stopped coming to the store, orders already placed for christenings and parties were canceled, and within weeks I had no choice but to close the doors of Exotic Touch.

As the daughter of a mobster, I have lived the good and bad sides of the role. I have been indulged in the glitz and the glamour befitting a Mafia princess. But I have also experienced the downside, the fear that comes with living in a house of cards.

Growing up, I was high on a pedestal. I enjoyed the attention and respect that came with being the daughter of a Mafia boss. But when I fell, it was a long way down. The in-between was just not there for me. When my father cooperated, I was still a kid trying to find my way, even if I was nineteen. I had always been coddled and protected. I was just emerging from my little cocoon and suddenly I had to survive on my own. Now I was trying to figure out who I really was and where in this new world I belonged.

It was such a critical point in my development. I didn't know how to move forward, it felt like having your wheels stuck in deep, thick mud. I knew that people were judging me because of who my father was. Although people never said it to my face, they said it behind my back. My girlfriends never made me feel that way. They always had my back. The kids I hung out with in the schoolyard had it, too, believe it or not. I really didn't care at this point what everyone else thought, as long as

I had my girlfriends and some loyal friends at the schoolyard. Dad's friends backing away from us was starting to mean less and less to me. I had my own group of people that cared about me.

My rebellion against my father and his entire way of life started now.

CHAPTER FOURTEEN

"The most significant witness in the history of organized crime in the United States."

Mom sent out a message to everyone she knew saying we were not a part of my father's decision in the slightest and that we were not going into witness protection. We communicated with my father by phone, but we stopped all visits. From time to time, I would still see the agents who had arrested my father drive past the house. They would drive by slowly, making sure I saw them if I was outside. Now that my father was gone, I always wondered why they continued to watch us. It was like they were doing it to bother me. But Dad later told me that the agents who had had him under surveillance for years had grown fond of him. They were the same guys who had watched me sneak out of the house all those times, and with Dad in prison, they felt an obligation to protect us.

When Dad and I did speak on the phone, our conversations

were very superficial. I was sincere when I told him I missed him. I really and truly did. I didn't want to hurt him, either. But I was *very* angry and confused and said a lot of hurtful things anyway.

Now that my father's secret life was being played out in the media, I just zoned out. I was in a state of total rebellion, I spent the next several months partying my ass off in New York City. I went to clubs, drank, danced, and smoked weed to excess. My mother tried talking to me, but I tuned her out. My friends weren't concerned about what my father had done. They looked at me as me, and that felt good.

Four months after my father cooperated, John Gotti's trial got under way. I tried to block the whole thing out, hard as it was. John had asked Mom to come to court and sit in on the proceedings to distract my father when he was testifying. She said she couldn't do it, and John understood. This wasn't her lifestyle on trial, and she was staying away.

My mother, Gerard, and I went to California for the duration of the proceedings. I didn't want to be in New York, opening up the newspaper every day and seeing a picture of my father with a rat's head on it. It really bothered me to see that picture. I knew in my heart that my father wasn't cooperating because he was scared of going to jail for the rest of his life, yet that's what people were saying about him. I understood that it was way deeper than what it looked like to the outside world, yet I did the right thing and said nothing.

John had a reputation for tampering with the jury, so all the jurors were sequestered for the monthlong trial. The news was calling it the Trial of the Century. Prosecutors were calling my father "the most significant witness in the history of organized crime in the United States."

My father was on the witness stand for nine grueling days. Although my mother did not agree to sit in the courtroom to intimidate Dad, Joey D'Angelo, the son of Dad's best friend Stymie, had agreed to be in the front row of the gallery the day my father took the stand. Dad was steamed at John Gotti for bringing the kid to the trial. My father had always been torn about bringing Joey into the life. This wasn't the path that most of the men wanted for their children, but after Stymie died, Joey was stuck to my father like glue and looked up to Dad like a father figure. Dad worried that if he chased him away, Joey would find another way to get into the life, so he had taken him under his wing, Dad's way of keeping him close.

Dad knew that Gotti had asked Joey to come to court to stare him down. John was doing everything he could to break my father. At one point during Dad's nine days on the stand, a woman came into the courtroom screaming that Sammy had killed her sons. Dad didn't even know who she was; he'd never seen her before. All of a sudden court deputies were racing to tackle the woman.

But Dad was unflappable, and remained stoic throughout the trial. Every time John tried to break him, it only made him stronger.

On April 2, 1992, after fourteen hours of deliberations, the jury found John Gotti guilty on thirteen counts of murder and various other crimes. Frank Locascio was found guilty of conspiracy to murder and of money laundering, among other things. The judge who presided over the cases, Leo Glasser, called my father's testimony "the bravest thing" he had ever seen. Both John and Frank were sentenced to life in prison without the possibility of parole. Gotti was flown to the United States Penitentiary at Marion, Illinois, where he spent most of his sentence in solitary confinement until he died of throat cancer on June 10, 2002. Frankie went to a federal prison in Terre Haute, Indiana, but was moved to the Federal Medical Center in Devens, Massachusetts, in April 2010.

Dad's testimony also helped send thirty-seven other members of organized crime to prison, among them Gambino crime family bosses and high-ranking members of the Genovese, Colombo, and DeCavalcante crime families.

After the Gotti trial, Mom, Gerard, and I returned to Staten Island. Dad remained in protective custody in a federal facility and was later sent to Phoenix, Arizona. He was not formally sentenced until September 1994. By then, he had already served most of his five-year sentence, which was to be followed by three years of controlled release.

I was a lot like my father, but it was impossible to wrap my head around what he had done. I also couldn't ignore the hurtful things being whispered about my family. Even Aunt Fran and Uncle Eddie were distancing themselves from us.

For a time, I continued to live at home in Staten Island. I was still a teenager and cared deeply about my image and what other people thought about me. I was confused about the choice my father had made. The more articles that came out about him, the more rebellious I became, and the more I felt I had something to prove. Mom was also feeling the rejection. Her friends had been distancing themselves from her, and she, in turn, started withdrawing. People were afraid of what others might think if they were seen hanging around with us. People who owed my father money just walked away. It wasn't right.

Oddly, my brother, Gerard, wasn't shunned. He was younger than me and his friends in the neighborhood didn't seem to care about Dad's cooperation one way or the other. He continued to hang out with his friends and went about his normal routine. His friends weren't old enough to be wannabes yet. And a lot of his friends' parents weren't connected. But I was still struggling with that ridiculous question that wouldn't leave me alone: which person was I, the upstanding one or the sinister one? I had a choice to make. I could divorce myself from "the life" and start a new one for myself.

I felt more comfortable being bad. That was my father's world, and even though it was an ominous one, it gave me some sense of safety and protection. I was comfortable in its familiarity. With a false sense of invincibility, I began to channel my father as I wound my way through the New York City street life.

In my heart, I had wanted to divorce myself from the decision my father had made to cooperate. The criminal life came so easily to me. I didn't realize it, but I was carrying on my father's legacy. I didn't know any other way. My sole purpose was to try to regain for myself the respect my father had squandered. I was convinced that being bad was the only way. I put on this tough girl persona. It was my way of blocking out what was going on inside me. The truth was I was mad at my father, but I was still missing him. I felt angry and confused.

I didn't mind when the flower shop closed. I didn't think I was cut out to be a florist anyway. I went to St. John's University in Staten Island for a semester, but I dropped out. Tommy and I had broken up after three years and I had a new boyfriend, Lee D'Avanzo, the leader of our neighborhood crew. He had a reputation as a real bad boy. I felt that if I was with him, nobody was going to say shit about me.

Lee was tall, with a very dark complexion and big, olive-shaped brown eyes. He was handsome, and he had this certain toughness that I was attracted to, he had a leadership quality in him. He was three years older than me, and he lived a couple of blocks away from the schoolyard where we hung out.

I'd known Lee for years. My father had actually saved his life when he was younger. Back when I was dating Tommy, Dad had come home from the gym one day and asked me to get him something out of his gym bag. Inside the bag, he had a list with three names. One of them was Lee's.

"Why do you have these names?" I asked him.

My dad said, "Do you know these kids?"

I answered, "I do."

We started talking specifically about Lee.

My dad inquired, "Is he a good kid?"

I had heard things he had done, like stealing hubcaps and other stuff from cars. I knew he was a tough kid. He had been raised by his mother, after his car-thief father was killed by the Feds outside a chop shop. He found out about it when he was a kid, just coming in from trick-or-treating one Halloween.

Everybody in the house was crying. He asked his mother what time his father would be back, and she said never, and not to mention his name again. Eventually, Lee found out about the shootout and hated the Feds and the government for what they had done to his family. He became the breadwinner at a very young age, and his mother looked the other way as long as money was coming in.

Dad didn't know any of this history, but if I knew Lee, that was good enough for him. He said, "Do me a favor, can you get this kid to come and see me tomorrow? Tell him not to leave his house until he comes to see me."

I called Tommy and asked him if he could reach out to Lee, and have him come to my house. Lee and Tommy knew each other from the schoolyard. They ran in a mutual crowd. Lee got the message, and showed the next day. Lee had been in a fight a couple of days earlier and had beaten up a wiseguy's nephew. This wiseguy had put a hit out on Lee. He wanted to send a message to the Springville boys, to let them know that if they were going to be on the streets running around, they needed to know there was a code. My father explained that Lee and his friends had to be careful about who they beat up. They also had to answer to someone in organized crime, since the families ran the streets. Lee agreed, thanking my father for saving his life. After that, Lee seemed to watch out for me. He may have felt some sort of loyalty to Dad. A couple of years later we started dating.

Lee wasn't much for the city, so we hung out at clubs on Staten Island or in Brooklyn. On weekends, we'd go to Hunter Mountain or the Hamptons. At this time the only thing that really mattered to me was my social life. Once in a while, I'd talk to Dad on the phone, but I was pretty much living it up to get him out of my mind. My mother was worried about my reckless behavior, but I shrugged off her concern.

By this point, Lee and I were pretty serious. We had been dating for nearly two years. Dad was serving his sentence in Arizona. My mother spoke to Dad regularly to keep him updated on the family. I didn't visit him, but I spoke to him on the phone from time to time. Not long after one of their conversations, Mom announced that we were moving to Arizona. The FBI had visited Dad in prison and told him they had credible information that there was a possible hit on Gerard's life, so she wanted to get us out of New York.

The Feds didn't want to give Dad too much information

because they didn't want my father to retaliate as soon as he got released. John Gotti had not sanctioned the hit. No matter what his relationship was with my father, he always conducted himself like a man when it came to me, my mother, and Gerard. He never took it out on us that my father cooperated. If anything, he made sure we were protected to the best of his ability. He would never have wanted any of us to be hurt. He was not like that. He knew the rules and would never cross them when it came to women and children. Besides, the FBI would have been all over him if something had happened. I think in his heart, John could never accept what my father did, but he knew who Dad was, and he knew why he did what he did. I don't know what the motive was behind the hit out on my brother, probably to send a message to Sammy. Or maybe just same jerk trying to make a name for himself who might hurt Gerard to gain respect.

Agents told my father that the plan was for a good friend of Gerard's to lure him to a nightclub. There, a hit team would be waiting to take Gerard out. An associate of Dad's had been the one to stop it. Dad had once saved the man's life, and he felt it was his obligation to make sure nothing ever happened to any of our family. We heard that the guy threatened to personally kill anyone who touched one hair on Gerard's head. Even though Dad had cooperated, he still had a lot of loyal friends on the street. There were a lot of people he did not hurt, people he did not testify against, people he would simply not go against, period.

Dad reached out to Mom to discuss the whole mess. They appreciated the protection, but feared Gerard would always be targeted. He would always live in the shadow of The Bull.

My parents decided the best thing to do was to move us out

of New York. Mom chose Arizona because she had visited there once before and had liked it. Gerard was eighteen and just out of high school, and Phoenix was a hopping college town, perfect for someone Gerard's age. My aunt Diane was newly divorced, so relocating sounded good to her, too. Mom, Gerard, Gerard's girlfriend Maria, Aunt Diane, and her two kids, Gina and Anthony, were ready to make the big move. Mom said she liked the warm climate and slower pace of life in the southwest.

Mom bought a nice, spacious house outside of Phoenix, and Aunt Diane bought the one directly next door. They even opened up the backyards to join the properties. My mother had a friend who knew of someone who had a business for sale, a bagel store in Tempe, near Arizona State University. She thought she and Gerard could run it.

Gerard was okay with the idea. He wasn't sure what he would do in Arizona, but he wanted to be with our mother. I, on the other hand, refused to move with them. I was a tried-and-true New Yorker, I told them, and I had no intention of leaving town.

Lee and I were going strong, I was having a great time, and once in a while I even forgot that my father was in prison. The house on Lamberts Lane was empty with Mom and Gerard gone. They had packed up and shipped a lot of the stuff to Arizona, leaving me with just the essentials and my stuff. I invited Lee to move in with me. At the time, he owned his own house on Staten Island, so he sold that and brought his belongings. He was a bank robber, so I didn't really need to work. He was stealing enough money for both of us.

Lee was committing crimes, and I was trying to figure out a career for myself. Mom had left me some money, and Lee took care of most of the bills. He was out robbing and stealing in the evenings, so we always had plenty of money. I knew what he was doing but I still followed our family's code of not asking any questions. But Lee told me anyway.

I was pretty well taken care of. When I wasn't working, I'd be hanging with the girls, Ramona, Roxanne, and Jennifer. We'd go to the Palladium and the Limelight or any other place in New York City that was happening that night. Lee didn't like me going out with my friends. He was kind of controlling that way. But he was going out with his friends, and I was not the controllable type. Most of our arguments had to do with what time I got in. I never gave him shit when he was gone for days at a time to do his crimes.

One late July night, Lee and I were sleeping in my upstairs bedroom when bullets ripped through my window. This was no ordinary pane-glass window. It was something Dad had gone to great effort to have custom-made and installed. It was a forty-inch stained-glass circle with a huge letter G in the middle. The bullets flew right over the bed and lodged in the closet where we had once kept the safe with the money.

We had no idea why someone was shooting up the house, but I assumed it must have had something to do with my father. There was no way I was going to call the cops, and no one else in the neighborhood did either. Maybe nobody heard anything, because the house was right on the service road to the freeway, but more likely nobody wanted to get involved in gangster business.

The next morning, Lee and I went outside and saw that my gray Acura was shot up, too. The side panel had two bullet holes in it. I called my mother in Arizona and she called Uncle Eddie to look in on us. Uncle Eddie already knew about it, but he hadn't come to check on me. I'm not sure why not. Big Louie

Valario and Mikey Scars were two friends who were loyal to the family, and they started coming by the house to make sure I was okay after they heard about it. I still felt protected in this lifestyle, but I started to see this really wasn't what I wanted.

Lee took my car to a friend's body shop. The mechanic took out the bullets and patched up the holes. I never bothered to have the stained-glass window repaired. I just had the repairman replace it with clear glass. I didn't find out who did it until years later. It turned out it wasn't a retaliatory attack against Dad like I had thought. A kid from Staten Island was actually sending a message to Lee, because he didn't like him. This was a warning. Lee and I never talked about it, as weird as that might sound. We just brushed it off.

The house was already on the market when it got shot up. Lee and I had decided to move to Phoenix and try and make a new start there. We had been to visit Mom and Gerard and we liked it. Lee had been arrested a couple of times for fighting and was on the radar of the police, and I was missing my family. I didn't want to leave Lee, so we'd have to go together.

When I told Mom we were coming, she was elated. I was the one to show the house to perspective buyers until it was sold. It was really hard to turn it over to someone else. Dad had invested so much of his time and heart in this house, and so much of it was personal. This was where some of my fondest memories of my rebellious teenage years took place. For most of our time in Bulls Head, Dad had been the respected gangster that everybody knew. Our parties were legendary. We really belonged here.

Letting it go was heartbreaking. Mom came back for the closing. The house was in her name, so all the proceeds were hers, not my father's. To get the money to relocate to Arizona,

Mom also sold the office building on Stillwell Avenue, and other property that was also, conveniently, in her name. We packed up all the belongings still there that we wanted to keep, and gave the rest to family and neighbors. A lot of the furniture was Lee's, so we put it on the moving truck for our new place. The only part of the whole move that gave me any comfort was knowing I'd be back with Mom and Gerard.

CHAPTER FIFTEEN

"I'm not a punk and I'm not a fool."

Lee and I found a rental apartment in a suburb of Phoenix in the East Valley, around the corner from Mom. It was a spacious two-bedroom unit on the second level of a two-story complex. It had a gorgeous swimming pool landscaped with palm trees and a state-of-the-art gym for all the renters. The rent was dirt cheap, nothing like in New York. The setting was unbelievable. The city of Phoenix was totally flat, but surrounded by desert and mountains. Camelback Mountain was right in the middle of town. I had never seen such vegetation: huge cacti, weird-looking yucca, and lots of sagebrush. It never seemed to rain out there. Every day was cloudless, blue skies, with no humidity. The sunsets were incredible, shades of pinks and blues and other colors that I never saw in a New York sunset.

Lee had saved enough money for us to live on for a while

without worrying. The plan was to eventually buy a house and a business and stay in Arizona for good. For a short time, I worked at Manhattan Bagels, the bagel store Mom and Gerard were running in Tempe. Bagels were hard to come by in Arizona, and the town had lots of New York transplants, so Mom's shop was doing pretty well. Working there gave me a chance to get a feel for the area and to decide what kind of business we'd like to run.

My dream of a better life was beginning to come true. Lee and I were together in Arizona and we had plans to operate a real business. I didn't want to be married to someone with the "lifestyle," so I was hoping Arizona would be where I was going to live a normal life. But it didn't work out that way.

Lee couldn't make any money out there, so he was flying back to New York to make a buck. He even brought some guys from New York out to Arizona and they started doing crime there. He was drawn to criminal activity. He wasn't the working type; he liked the feeling of getting away with it.

Lee knew how to make money illegally, but he didn't know how to make it grow. He was nothing like my father. Even though Dad was the boss in every business he had, he didn't have a problem working. He still went to the office every day. My father liked to follow a structure. That quality was missing with the street guys of today, they didn't have structure.

My father was still in prison in Arizona when we first got out there, but he was getting out soon. While he had been in prison, I had started longing for a relationship with him. I had been to visit him once, which had been awkward. I missed him, but I was still so angry with him, I couldn't put it behind me.

Lee and I were still struggling to make it happen in Phoenix when my father was released in early 1995. He was immediately put into a federal witness protection program in Boulder, Colorado, where he was supposed to create a whole new life for himself.

Dad called me when he got out. My anger was beginning to subside and I was willing to begin to repair our relationship, but I didn't want to let my guard down one hundred percent. I was now in my twenties, and I felt like I had to prove my independence to him. I took his cooperation with the government very personally, I felt as though he had abandoned me, and his decision had changed my life's path. He was always hassling me to go to college and find a career for myself, but I didn't want to hear it. I would find something when I was ready. I knew that he was only doing it because he wanted me to have a better life. But I was standoffish. It wasn't my intention to hurt his feelings, but he had hurt mine. I was also still very upset with him for what I felt he had done to our family.

Finally, Lee and I went to visit my father outside of Boulder, Colorado, for a few days. This was a big deal for me. Dad had met Lee one other time, but now he was my boyfriend, so Dad viewed him in a different light. I knew he had heard lots of rumors. He had been informed by the Feds about what Lee did for a living and that Lee and I were together. They had come to my father while he was still in prison to tell him "your daughter is dating a street guy," and Dad understood what that meant.

It was really nice to make the trip. When Dad picked us up at the airport, he was wearing jeans and a jean jacket, not the sweats I was so accustomed to. Dad didn't do much to alter his appearance; he just had some minor plastic surgery to correct cartilage damage in his nose. He had started dressing differently in jeans and construction boots. The Feds had given him a completely new identity. They provided him with an alias,

Jimmy Moran, and registered a construction company in his name. It struck me as funny, my dad Sammy the Bull, Italian in every hair and DNA fiber in his body, purporting to be an Irishman. But there was no way he could lose his Brooklyn accent, his Italian heritage, and his passion for Sicilian cuisine.

Dad's apartment had a small balcony that looked over Boulder Creek, which ran right beside the backyard of the complex. He liked to sit out on his deck chair, sipping coffee and watching the water race by. He had a little dog, a miniature Doberman named Petie, to keep him company. The apartment was really nice, although not in the taste I was used to from Dad. He was so contemporary, and this place had a more country-western style, with wood furniture, dark tiles, and plaid curtains.

"How is it living here?" I asked him. I knew how he was always ready to remodel and redecorate, but this was a rental. "Is the apartment complex going to let you rip down walls?" I joked. I was talking about his eye for design and style.

Dad said he didn't care. He was adaptable and could live anywhere. All the reconstruction had always been for us, to make our lives more comfortable. "I always wanted the best for you," he answered. "I wasn't about blowing my money on broads and alcohol and flashy clothes, I wanted to give you guys a place where you could feel comfortable and people could come and hang out."

I finally got him to admit he was thinking a little about how he could remodel.

Dad seemed to be doing well living in Colorado. He was relaxed and happy. His mannerisms and his confidence were the same. There was nothing different in that way about the underboss gangster from back in New York. But it was clear that he was on a different path.

My father was very happy to see me, but I believed this visit was so he could talk to Lee, to find out what type of person he was, what his motives were, and how he was treating me. Although he didn't show it, I am sure Lee was nervous for a bunch of reasons, not the least of which was that he knew who my father was and what he was capable of. Dad could be intimidating in a calm way. He liked to joke, but he was a very serious man and very serious about his family. He was concerned about what roles and positions people were going to play in his life, especially now.

Dad took Lee and me out a lot over the four days we were there. We'd go out to eat or drive around seeing the local sights or the mountains, and even went out to a bar at night to drink. This was the first time I ordered an alcoholic beverage in front of him. The whole time, I knew my father was reading Lee. He was a master at reading people. Plus, he was very controlled. Those were skills he had been born with, but he had sharpened them in the Mafia. His were almost survival skills; he could acutely analyze people in a very controlled way.

Dad's apartment only had one bedroom, so he gave that room to Lee. He and I slept in the living room, him on the couch and me in a big chair. He already had a lot of insight into Lee's lifestyle, because that's the way he had started. He understood Lee was a street guy, but he also realized that he didn't have a full understanding of organized crime. Lee was more of a cowboy, he was untamable and didn't want to answer to anyone. But Dad wanted to know what Lee's intentions were for the future, was he willing to give up his ties to New York to be with me? Dad told Lee he was planning on leaving the witness protection program. He stated that his family chose not to go into the program, so he was going to sign himself out. He was going to go to Arizona and be there in the background to make sure his kids were okay, keeping his identity a secret. Since the threat on Gerard, he promised himself he would guard the family, even if it meant putting himself at risk. Besides, my father didn't like the constraints of the witness program. He wasn't free to move around as he pleased. There were too many rules and regulations and he didn't want to have to answer to it.

He had money stashed away and was going to use it to help the family, setting us up in legitimate businesses. He was as good a businessman as he was a gangster. He was ready to get his life back in order and was willing to help Lee if he was going to be with me.

He said, "If you are going to be with my daughter, I would like to interact with you. You can be successful. You can do it in business, and I can help you."

Lee agreed. Our final evening in Boulder was going better than I expected. Lee and my father seemed to be hitting it off and I was relieved. It had been a long day of touring, a very emotional four days, and I was tired. The men weren't ready to turn in so I went off to the bedroom for a good night's sleep, leaving Lee and my father in the living room talking.

When I was asleep, Dad gave Lee the talk. "I'm not a punk and I'm not a fool," he told Lee. "I was never scared to go to jail. I didn't cooperate 'cause I was scared. I never do anything half-assed. I might have walked away from that lifestyle but I did not change who I am."

My father basically told Lee that he was planning to move to Arizona, and if anyone were ever to come to Arizona to hurt

174

his family or anyone he loved, it would be a war. For my father to be able to accept Lee into his life, he would have to be certain whose side he was on. Dad was very serious about his family and protecting the ones he loved; he was also big on knowing people's loyalties, and he was testing Lee's now. Dad asked him a hypothetical question, if he would be willing to murder if my father asked him to. In this way, Dad determined that Lee was a street fighter and a criminal, but he was not a murderer.

I didn't know about any of this until four months later, but I didn't believe that Lee had any intention of crossing my father or me. Still, I think Dad's conversation made him uncomfortable. I think Lee realized that even though Dad had cooperated, he was still the same old Sammy and would stop at nothing to protect his family.

The next morning, Lee and I flew back to Phoenix. Lee became kind of distant after that. I just thought it was because he wasn't happy in Arizona. He was having trouble making a living when he wasn't in New York. He was already flying back and forth between New York and Phoenix, but he often mentioned he was longing to go back to Staten Island permanently.

I think Lee realized that if he were going to be around someone like Sammy the Bull, there was no room to mess up. After the conversation with Dad, he understood he would always be caught in the middle, and the middle wasn't a good place to be. That conversation in Boulder played a big role in how he wanted to move forward. Since he was going to be in New York, he needed to show that he had no connection to Sammy the Bull, even though he was with his daughter.

A couple of months after visiting my father in Boulder, Lee moved back to New York. True to his word, my father was leaving the witness protection program and moving to Phoenix, and Lee wanted to be gone before that happened. I stayed behind in Arizona for two months, and then joined Lee in Staten Island.

Lee and I rented a two-bedroom apartment in an elevator building. It was on Wellington Court, near La Tourette Park and the Staten Island Mall. We went out and bought all new couches, a kitchen table, and other furniture, rather than waste the money to ship everything back. Dad respected my wishes that I wanted to return to New York. He felt that he had gotten his message through to Lee when he told him if he was going to be with his daughter, he was going to protect and love me the same way Dad protected and loved me.

Dad later told me during the meeting in Boulder he had tested Lee to see if he had the ability to kill. He was reading him from every angle. If Lee was in Arizona to set him up, he wanted to know. Lee did not respect authority because of what had happened to his father, Dad said, and he was drawn to the criminal underworld, but he didn't understand Cosa Nostra. My father didn't view Lee as a threat to me, but he wanted better for me. He had a feeling that Lee was going to end up in prison.

After Lee and I got back to New York, our relationship was never the same. I believe the conversation he had with my father that night in Boulder played a key role in our troubles.

Lee basically told me he didn't want me to have contact with my father. But he knew I would never go along with it. From that point on, he and I never talked about my father or my relationship with him. I was starting to understand my father and was ready to rebuild our relationship. He was my father, and I missed him.

Back in New York, Lee and I were going through the motions

of being together, but we really weren't getting along. I think I just stayed with him because I felt comfortable and protected. I really had no contact with my family at that point, and Lee was the closest thing I had to family. However, he had a wicked temper, and he was very controlling.

No matter what our problems were, however, I still protected Lee, because I felt like he protected me. I knew the fighting wasn't right; and that true gangsters and true men didn't lose their cool with women. But I felt that in New York I had no one else to answer to, and I knew that Lee would keep me in check. Being with him gave me a sense of security while I was there.

After we got back to New York, the Feds updated my father a couple of times about Lee. They told him Lee was involved in bank robbery and was going to end up in serious trouble with the law some day. Dad was concerned about Lee's behavior. He worried that if our apartment was ever raided with me in there, we were at higher risk because of who my dad was. I would be in deep shit even though I wasn't doing anything, only because my last name was Gravano.

Dad told me he had always wanted better for me. He said Lee was a street kid and was always going to be a street kid, robbing and stealing to get by. He was never going to have millions of dollars hidden in the walls. He was always making money here and there, but it wasn't enough for a rainy day.

A lot of what Dad said made sense. Lee was conflicted about the relationship, too. He wanted to be in my life, but there was this underlying tension that had to do with my father. Lee had as many misgivings about my father as my father had about him. We were not a happy, loving couple, despite the four years we had been together, though we were not ready to let go.

M_y relationship with Lee grew toxic. He cheated on me, I cheated on him; it was bad. After one particularly angry blowout, I packed up my suitcase and moved to my grandmother's house on Fifteenth Avenue in Brooklyn. Grandma Scibetta wintered in Florida, so the place was vacant. I invited a new friend I'd made to move in with me, an Albanian girl named Drita Selmani.

Drita was dating a guy named Albert, a kid Lee knew from the streets. I had been out with Roxanne Rizzo the night we met. Drita tapped me on the shoulder and asked me if I knew this stripper girl. I said, "I know of her, but we're not friends." She said, "Good, because I am going to break her face." Drita was pissed because she believed this girl was banging her boyfriend. I didn't see what happened, but Drita later told me she beat the girl up right there inside the club. After that, we became fast friends.

I'd met Drita before Lee and I had moved to Arizona, and we stayed friends while I was in Phoenix, constantly talking on the phone. When I got back, we started hanging out all the time. She used to come over to our apartment on Wellington Court. Sometimes, the four of us, Lee, Albert, Drita, and I, would go on double dates together.

Like Lee and me, Drita and Albert were on a rocky road. If Lee and I had a fight, Drita was right there. She was my girl. I confided in her, hung out with her, and brought her around my other friends.

Roxanne and Ramona didn't like her that much. She wasn't with us since childhood and they didn't trust her. Her parents were Albanian immigrants, and she hadn't grown up in our neighborhood. She was raised very differently from us, but I thought Drita was cool. I wasn't the type to get caught up in petty girl gossip. I slowly integrated her into our circle.

After a couple of months living at my grandmother's, I moved back in with Lee. Drita moved back in with her parents on Staten Island. Lee was still covering all the bills, but I liked to stay independent, so I found a job answering phones for a Russian penny stock trader. I got Drita a job there, too.

It didn't take us long to figure out that the company wasn't legit. Everyone who worked there had a thick Russian accent and went by the name "Richard Smith." I was being paid eight hundred dollars a week in cash for my secretarial services. It was a good gig and they treated me well, but it was short-lived. I had only been there four months when I arrived for work one morning to find the place shuttered, cleaned out, and closed down. When my secretarial job with the Russians disappeared during the night, I started looking for something else to do.

My fights with Lee were escalating, so to escape the yelling I started to spend more time at my childhood friend Jennifer Graziano's apartment in Manhattan. Jenn was breaking up with her boyfriend, and I was at the end of my rope with Lee, so we found comfort in each other.

Jennifer was a brainiac. She was taking classes at New York University's Stern School of Business, working on credits toward a master's degree. She lived in an apartment on Thirty-ninth Street in Manhattan while she was in school. I was there all the time, only going home once in a while to sleep at night.

Jenn had lived the same kind of life I had lived until my father cooperated. She even had a mother a lot like mine, a very devoted mother, a typical Mafia wife, ask no questions, see no evil, just take care of your family. They kept our homes, cooked our meals, and raised and cared for us kids. They had no external ambitions for themselves, just to make sure their families were happy.

Now I needed a way to support myself, and that's where my friend, whom I will call Christina, came in handy. Like me, Christina's father had mob associations. She also had a boyfriend who was running a marijuana delivery service, and she had been helping him out. But when she had found out he'd been cheating on her, she was so furious that she had stolen and copied his customer list and wanted to start her own business. Did I want to help?

At that point, I thought it sounded perfect. I didn't like taking money from Lee. I wanted to be independent.

We set up our new enterprise with all the props of a legitimate business. We printed up business cards and called ourselves herbalists. We sent a mailing, alerting her boyfriend's clients that his delivery service had changed its name to Aromatherapy, the name of our newly founded operation.

"Let us *lift* your mind with our *herbs*, flowers and *trees* straight from the land of *Buddha.* Our *herbalists* will take you to *higher* levels and help you kick back and relax with our *Aromatherapy*," the cards read, using innuendoes and street slang used by smokers.

Christina's boyfriend, now her ex, went nuts. Our service hired all girls.

Christina was the brains. She was able to organize the operation like a business. We had computers, codes, beepers, and coded mail-outs. I was the action, I did the running. I hit the streets and did the legwork. I did not fear getting robbed, knocking on doors, or making deliveries. I said to myself, "I'm bad, I can do this." I had no fear.

I was still living with Lee, but he had no idea what I was up to. I didn't want him to find out because Christina and I were trying to keep a low profile so our fathers wouldn't find out what we were doing. The one criminal activity the Mafia looked down on was drug dealing. Most people thought Cosa Nostra was big into narcotics dealing, but that was not the case. The Federal RICO Act had strict subjective sentencing guidelines for drug crimes, and had mandatory sentences of twenty or more years with no room for plea bargaining. It wasn't worth it to lose a man for that kind of time.

Our business took off immediately. We couldn't even keep up with the demand. For the first time in a long time, I was having fun and felt as though I was on top of the world. I was dealing with prominent Puerto Rican gang members and other street kids, but I felt I could hold my head up again. I had become my own person, Gina, the marijuana dealer. It made me feel like I was gaining respect.

CHAPTER SIXTEEN

"There's a rumor that Sammy's daughter
is running a weed service."

It had been my decision to be a drug dealer. I went from being Meadow Soprano in the HBO hit series *The Sopranos* to Nancy Botwin of *Weeds*. I became the consummate pusher, on call twenty-four hours a day. The money was rolling in, and Christina and I were spending it just as fast. We were going to clubs, getting tables right next to all the up-and-coming rap and hip-hop superstars like Puffy and Biggie, and drinking expensive top-shelf bottles of champagne. We became known as the "Mafia girls." Everyone thought we had money because our fathers were gangsters. Little did they know, we were earning it all on our own. I was completely seduced by being in the limelight and got caught up in the celebrity of it all.

I felt like I was the queen of the universe. I was living in New York and running a marijuana delivery service. As strange as it might seem to those who have only led a legitimate life, I felt I'd regained respect in the streets. My father never sold drugs; he was against them, as most people in the Mafia were. I felt like I was separating myself from his lifestyle and making my own place in a different kind of underworld.

I took pride in being a drug dealer, making my own money and having people look up to me. I was starting to mimic the lifestyle of my father in his early years. I think that is what happens when you have a strong father figure who is really powerful, you mimic him. I have had guys tell me it is hard to deal with me because I am very strong-minded. I am not a submissive girl. I felt so much pressure after Dad cooperated that I wanted to be bad.

Christina and I were more scared of getting caught by our fathers than by the cops. We had this secret, this sisterhood, and this loyalty to each other.

One week, Christina was away on vacation, and I was running everything by myself. Christina and I opened at noon and we closed at midnight, so I was on a tight schedule, running around answering the phones, packaging the weed, and delivering it all by myself. Lee had become highly suspicious of my nights out, and he had decided to follow me. He watched me run up and down the stairs to five different drops in five different apartment buildings, staying at each for a good half hour to make sure the customer was satisfied with the weed and to get the money. I had just left the fifth building when, as I turned the corner, there came Lee. I had a pouch on my waist with cylinders filled with weed. Some were filled with fifty-dollar higher-grade stuff like Purple Haze and Kush. Others were thirty-dollar bags with mid-grade quality.

"What are you doing?" he yelled.

I didn't want him to know I was working in the drug delivery business. He was a criminal, why did I care? But you don't want your girl doing crime, too. I got all nervous and started stumbling. Lee went to grab my pouch and all the weed spilled out onto the sidewalk.

"Are you sick?" he yelled at me, both amused and not amused at the same time. "I thought you were a prostitute. I was following you from building to building."

"I'm a weed dealer," I replied.

"What do you mean you're a weed dealer?" he said. He went on to say if that was the case, maybe he could help me out with contacts.

I stayed with Lee for about a year and a half after that, but our fights were becoming more and more volatile to the point where I couldn't take it anymore. A couple of months after he caught me dealing, I picked up and flew to Arizona on a whim.

I decided I wanted to go to skin school, so I stayed with my mother and enrolled in a beauty school to get an aesthetician's license. I figured that way I could take care of myself and use my license anywhere. Christina knew I would be back.

After four months in Phoenix, I had forgotten the bad stuff and the problems with Lee and couldn't stay away. I moved back into Wellington Court, excited for a fresh start. It soon became clear that our relationship wasn't going to work out, as we picked up right where we had left off. I tried to spend as much time away from the apartment as I could, but I realized that I needed to go. Once and for all, I officially moved out.

Jennifer was now living in Bayside, Queens, and she invited me to move into her two-bedroom condominium. Jenn was still in school, and I picked up with Christina in our weed business right where I'd left off.

As our business grew, Christina and I talked of expanding. We worked really well together; we were like a power team. Neither one of us had a big ego, so we didn't step on each other's toes.

When I got back to New York, I reconnected with a guy named Dave Seabrook. I had met him in January 1997, right before I moved out to Arizona to go to skin school. I had been partying with my girlfriends at the China Club, our favorite hangout in Times Square, where there were always celebrities from music, sports, fashion, and Broadway in the mix. Dave was there in the company of Jam Master Jay from the hip-hop band Run DMC. I was out to promote my new weed service and handed him a sample bag of Chronic, a high-end weed, to test out.

"You should try this," I told him. "It's Purple Haze. It's good."

"You're giving it to me?" Dave asked, puzzled.

I gave him a business card. "My name is Gina and there's more where that came from."

Dave called me the next day.

"Do you want to buy anything?" I asked.

"No, I just want to hang out," he said.

Dave was African American, handsome, and well dressed. I knew my father would greatly disapprove. Italians really preferred their kids to date their own kind. Dave wasn't the most upstanding citizen, not even by my standards. He was an ex-street hustler who'd just gotten out of jail after serving six years for robbery and attempted murder.

Dave had been born and raised in Hollis, Queens. It was a tough neighborhood, and a lot of the kids were into crime. He was sixteen when he and his cousin robbed a store. When they were running away, an off-duty cop tackled his cousin. According to Dave, the kid pulled a gun on the cop, but the officer was unable to pinpoint which of the two had done it. Dave went on the run for over a year, but was finally caught. He refused to implicate his cousin, so he was charged as an adult with attempted murder.

He spent six and a half years in various prisons in the New York State prison system. It wasn't his first time behind bars. He had already spent two years in a juvenile facility, so he was used to being locked up. Most of the kids in his neighborhood ended up in prison at one time or another.

I didn't care. I was doing everything that was as anti my father as possible. I was dealing drugs, partying, dating bad boys, and having a great time. Dave was different from the other guys I knew. He had a kind of swagger I had not seen before, and I was intrigued by him. He had grown up differently than I had, he'd been raised in a different culture and I was attracted to "different" at that time. We'd joke about what we called pasta, I said macaroni, Dave said noodles. The relationship was fresh. It fit into what I was doing.

I was selling weed and now I had this boyfriend fresh home from the penitentiary. Dave was gangster in a different way. He was more street hood.

Dave ran with his own crew. He never tried to take me on a date to Sparks Steak House, where all the gangster wannabes still hung out, despite the assassination of Paul Castellano outside of the restaurant more than a decade before. Dave wasn't very demanding, my new gold standard in a relationship after how controlling Lee had been.

Dave fit into my lifestyle. I didn't want anything serious, and he was fine with that. He was friends with hip-hopper Jam

Master Jay and had many contacts in the music industry, and he was really fun to be with. Likely, he knew a lot of people and could help us sell some weed, so that was good.

Christina and I were buying the good stuff from Spanish Harlem and the medium-quality weed from Staten Island. I felt like I had a different kind of control over my life than I had ever had before. There was a consistency to my days, which were orchestrated by me alone. I didn't feel like the Mafia princess I had been when I was a little girl. Then, people had looked at me like royalty. I'd go to restaurants and get silver spoon service because of who my father was.

Now, I felt like a boss. Christina and I had jumped into a whole new kind of bad. We were dealing with gangsters, but they didn't wear suits like John Gotti had. Christina and I were holding our own, getting respect from these people and I liked it.

We'd been running the weed service for less than two years when I started to feel lonely. I had accepted that Lee and I were done. Although I had friends that were like sisters to me, I still missed my family. It just wasn't the same. Ramona was rarely around. She was in a serious relationship with a Jorda-nian guy named Wally. Her family did not approve of the rela-tionship for many reasons, and she was caught up in her own problems. Although I was always there to help her, she was traveling extensively with her new boyfriend, who had busi-ness outside of the country.

Once again, I found myself caught between two worlds. Even though I was dating Dave, whom I cared a lot about, and had my girlfriends around me, I still very much needed my family. It was ironic that though I was leading the street life, the life I thought I wanted so badly, I still missed my family. I was living in a kind of dreadful limbo; I had no comfort zone.

I felt like I was on the outside again, this time not with my father's organized crime family, but with my own family. They weren't calling me anymore. I wasn't sure if that was their plan, to kind of cut me off and make me feel lonely. I had never asked them to stop calling, but I was missing them more.

While I was angry with my father, I realized that in many ways I was just like him. I found myself running my own criminal enterprise and I took pride in it. I was gaining respect on my own outside the lifestyle he had chosen. I'd lived in Brooklyn, Staten Island, and Manhattan and liked the fast pace, the nightlife, and the hustle and bustle of New York City. Besides, I had built a lucrative business for myself, even if it was illegal. Although I knew I always wanted more than that, I was caught in the moment and couldn't bring myself to shut it down.

Dad had done everything he told us he was going to do back when I had visited him in Boulder. He had remained in Colorado for only six months before leaving the witness protection program to join my mother and brother in Arizona.

Once my father relocated to Phoenix, he was no longer officially under the wing of the U.S. Marshals Service. He also had a long list of parole conditions he had to abide by. My dad didn't want my mother to be in any kind of danger on account of him, so he took his own apartment a short distance away in case somebody with a gun and a grudge came looking for him. My parents never lived together again after our house on

Lamberts Lane. They had actually gotten a divorce, but it was more for legal reasons than because of a bad marriage. Dad still called my mother his wife. They adored each other.

My parents had been through a lot in their marriage, but my mother was a very loyal person and no matter what my father's life had been and no matter what he had put her through as a wife, he had always been a good husband and a good father. My mother knew that it was never my father's intention to ever hurt her or their kids. She understood that he loved us and would protect us until the day he died. He had always been a good provider and made sure my mother was always well taken care of. She knew that no matter what decisions he had made in his world, he had always been good to us in our world.

Whenever I would call my family in Arizona, Mom would tell me that she, Dad, and my brother were going out for dinner or to a movie. They sounded like they were doing just fine without me. Dad even sounded like he had found a replacement for me. He had taken a real liking to a young college girl about my age named Jen. He had even hired her to work for him as his assistant at the construction business he was now running. Dad would never sink so low as to out-and-out compare me to her, but he'd say things like "she's a brainiac" or "she's going places," things that definitely made me feel judged or resentful. "I really want you to meet her," he would say, as if I wanted to make the acquaintance of somebody he thought more highly of than me.

I hadn't been out to Arizona for a while, so I decided to go back for a visit. While I was there, I met Dad's assistant, Jen. She was definitely from the west. She didn't have that city edge. Nothing she owned had a designer label, but I felt very intimidated by her. She wasn't chic, but she had an aggressive smartness. Dad was right. She was going to be somebody some day.

College didn't mean anything to me. I was now making three thousand dollars a week, without a college degree. Nevertheless, I felt I wasn't in Jen's league. She made me jealous.

Growing up, Dad had always looked at me and told me I was going to be somebody, a doctor or a lawyer or some other distinguished career. Now, on my trip to Arizona, he wasn't looking at me with that "I believe in you, you're going to make me proud" look. I think he'd given up on me. And for the first time, he wasn't insisting that I visit. It didn't seem to matter to him one way or another.

My parents had done everything they could for me and saw my life in a way that I couldn't. I was too entrenched in thinking that making money was all that mattered. I didn't care how I made it, as long as it was flowing in.

Once the visit was over and I was back in New York, I started to feel depressed and inadequate. A lot of our customers were professionals, the doctors and lawyers who my father once had dreamed I would be, except for their pot-smoking habits. When I visited their apartments, I found myself wondering what it would be like to have what they had: prestige, a nice place to live, and a respectable career.

To top it off, the kids from my old neighborhood were really running around trying to be gangsters now, no more hubcaps and petty stuff. It was because of the gangster life that my family was broken, that my father had gone to prison, that mother was living in another state across the country, and that my brother had avoided a hit on his life only because Dad's friend had been in the right place at the right time. I was homesick for my family.

Not only that, I had terrible guilt about something that had happened to Gerard. I had asked my brother to overnight me a pound of weed from Arizona and he got arrested for sending it. He dropped it at a mailing station, all wrapped up in newspaper, under brown paper and secured with packing tape, and addressed to New York. The female clerk thought he looked suspicious, so after he paid and left, she opened the package and found the weed. She didn't know how to locate him and there was no return address on the package. The next day, when I called him to say the package hadn't arrived, he called there to see when it had been sent. The same clerk star-sixty-nined him to get his phone number. Then, she called the police.

The cops called my brother and told him he had to turn himself in. Gerard reached out to Dad, and my father found him an attorney in Phoenix. Gerard ultimately beat the rap because the woman had opened the package without a warrant, so it was an illegal search and seizure. However, my father was furious with Gerard. My brother had a house, a restaurant, and a son, so Dad viewed his marijuana bust as reckless and irresponsible.

Gerard never told my father that the package had been for me. He abided by the family code of no tattling, work it out between you. My father knew Gerard and I dabbled in little things, but he wasn't aware of my drug business. Even though I hadn't gotten in trouble, being a party to my brother's arrest was a low point for me.

But the final straw came the day I went to a magazine, where a few of my clients were employed, to make a delivery. There were already rumors out there that Sammy the Bull's daughter was running a weed service. One of our clients, an editor at the magazine who knew me as "Gina," saw me when I came in. We had become friends, and we would talk for a bit whenever I came by.

But when I was leaving that day, he startled me when he didn't call me by my alias. "All right, Miss Gravano," he said. "See you next time."

"All right, bye," I said, starting for the door before turning back to him in total surprise. "Wait, what did you say?"

"There's a rumor that Sammy's daughter is running a weed service."

"I'm not her," I insisted.

"All right, Karen. Can I call you Karen?" The situation was making me uncomfortable. "Look, I don't know why you are doing this," he said. "You can be so much more." It turned out he was being protective. He told me to be careful. He thought I could be doing something better with my life. "If they catch you, they will lock you up and throw away the key simply because of your last name," he warned.

I thought I'd been doing such a good job of making sure nobody knew my family's history, but the combination of the fame and stigma associated with being a Gravano would follow me wherever I went. It had never occurred to me that I could have a conventional life. But my friend's comments got me thinking.

Besides, the drug business wasn't a career without its risks. Running the weed service had become increasingly dangerous. First of all, there were other services competing with ours. Everyone had been calling us because we were an all-girl service. But now customers were calling two services at a time and buying from whichever runner arrived first. Some of our runners were getting robbed. People started robbing each other. One night, Christina was held up at knifepoint as I stood by. Thankfully, we were just robbed and nobody got hurt. It scared the shit out of us.

We thought the best idea was to bring some muscle on board. Dave and some of his friends started watching our backs. Dave wasn't like my other boyfriends, who had been obsessed with the Mafia and the lifestyle. It didn't seem to matter to him. I liked that. It made the relationship about me, not Dad.

Getting the guys into the mix only led to more drama and confrontation and made the fights worse. When we were an all-girl service, no one would mess with us, but now all bets were off.

One night, we were at a nightclub and an altercation broke out. The cops ended up wanting to talk to Christina. They had heard the altercation was over our weed service. Although Christina was brought down to the station for questioning, she refused to talk to the officers. She wasn't being charged with anything, so they had to let her go.

Our biggest fear wasn't the cops; it was our fathers. We did not want our fathers to find out what we were doing. We knew how disappointed they would be.

The last of the fun was over, though. We were having too many close calls with one thing or another. I was beginning to realize that as much as I wanted to blame my father for everything that ever went wrong in my life, the time had come for me to accept responsibility for the results of my actions. It was time for me to grow up.

CHAPTER SEVENTEEN

"Do you have any remorse now?"

One morning I woke up and decided I was just done with New York. I was twenty-seven, missing my family, and confused about what I wanted. Christina had a college degree, so she had lots of options besides the weed business. I knew I couldn't go on this way forever. Eventually, I was going to get caught, so in October 1998, I joined my family in Phoenix. This was to become my new world and a fresh start for all of us, now that Dad was living there too. As a family, the Gravanos had been through so much heartache, pain, and betrayal. I was looking forward to some healing.

It was crazy to think back how at one point I had been asked to suggest to my father that he should kill himself, and even more crazy to not have even questioned that directive, total insanity. But conversations like that had been normal back then. Now I was in search of a different kind of normal.

Jennifer thought I was just going to Phoenix for a visit and would be coming back soon to her apartment in Bayside, being the consummate New Yorker that I was. When I first got out to Arizona, even I was convinced it was only temporary. My options were wide open. I had every intention of returning to New York, or maybe going to live in Los Angeles.

My mother picked me up at the airport. Dad greeted me at the curb when we pulled up in front of Mom's gorgeous new house that first day. After Dad had arrived from Boulder, he had bought my mother a new house and remodeled it to be 4,500 square feet, complete with an in-ground pool, so she would be comfortable. He had his own apartment somewhere nearby and had come around just for my return.

"Welcome home, kiddo," he beamed. "We have your room all ready for you. Do you want to see it?"

"I'm not staying forever," I responded. "This isn't my home."

He looked at me like he wanted to rip me a new asshole right then, but he said nothing. Gerard and his new baby were waiting for me, too. His girlfriend Mallory had given birth to their son, Nicholas, that past May, and I was so excited to get to know him. I hadn't seen him since I had flown out to Phoenix for his birth five months earlier. My brother had been keeping me up-to-date about all of the baby's milestones.

As much as I wanted to be happy, I couldn't allow myself to feel good. I didn't know how to let go of my anger and just fit back in. I was nasty, sarcastic, and confrontational.

We had dinner. I felt completely at home, but I didn't want to tell my parents that.

After dinner, Dad said, "Come on, let's go for a walk." He

had planted a rose garden in the backyard with a little bench in it. "You ever seen *The Godfather*," he asked me, "when Michael Corleone is in the rose garden?"

Why was he asking me this? I wondered.

"I know how hard it is to move here. I miss New York, too. But please trust me. I want to move on, and give you and your brother a chance in your life. If I can do that, if I can provide a new path, it will make me happy."

I didn't want to hear that. I just wanted him to be Sammy the Bull, the gangster.

"I know you think I've changed, but to be honest with you, I will always be Sammy," Dad continued. "I don't think you understand who Sammy is. I don't have to be in New York with people driving me around and on some pedestal to be who I am. I am trying to make a new path."

Dad took out a gun to show me. "I'm always going to be Sammy," he said. "I haven't changed. I'm still who I am."

I think he was trying to say that even though he was living outside the Mafia world, he hadn't changed. If his enemies were going to come after him, and this was his destiny, he was ready for it. But this was not his focus. His focus was getting everybody back on track and helping us to rebuild our lives.

"I am not a coward, I am not going to run," he said. "I am going to be right here banging it out 'cause this is who I am.

"I understand from the way you grew up that you think there's no other way," Dad said. He was trying to show me that there were opportunities for me outside New York. But I couldn't see it yet. I was still standoffish and not as open-minded about starting a new life. My answers to him were still a little snippy.

He should have checked me right there. My father had never allowed me to talk to him like that but I think he sat back as a parent and let me play out my anger. Only part of me had wanted to come to Phoenix, another part wasn't ready.

Dad wanted to keep me busy and not thinking about New York. The following morning, he showed up at Mom's house and took me shopping for a full aesthetician's setup. He got me a bed, steamer, table, and everything I would need to do facials in Mom's house in the room where Gerard had stayed. My brother had moved out and was living with his girlfriend and their new baby a couple of houses away from us. A couple of days later, I found a job at a local day spa, doing facials and body treatments.

Dad's small one-bedroom apartment was in a neighboring town. He lived there with his new dog, Petie Boy, who he had picked up after his first dog Petie fell off the balcony to his death in Boulder. Neither my mother nor my father ever moved on romantically, but they never really got back together again as a couple. Still, they remained friends. They were both living in Phoenix, but in separate households. My father felt it was important to be around us, but he also felt the need to keep his distance.

I was in Phoenix a little over a week when Dad and I hashed it out over dinner. We went out to his favorite Italian restaurant, just the two of us. The place was cute, and kind of hidden in an old house in Tempe, not far from the college. I had told Mom and Gerard I wanted to have dinner with Dad alone. I had so many questions, some I had wanted to ask him since I was very young. He was the one to break the code of silence first, so now I felt I could ask him anything I wanted, including those things my mother had so respectfully kept private.

"I don't want you to talk to me like you are Sammy the Bull or

Jimmy Moran. I want you to talk to me like you're my father," I told him unapologetically.

I asked him what it was like to kill someone. His response absolutely floored me.

"Surprisingly, the first time, it was a rush," he said. "It was just the craziest feeling because I didn't have remorse. I just felt empowered."

"Do you have remorse now?" I asked.

"I don't regret who I am. Although there are things I didn't like that I had to do in my life, I know why I did them and I have to live with them, so to answer your question I don't live with remorse, I live with reality and how to move past it. I chose that life. And if I needed to, I can kill someone tomorrow. I am trying to follow a new path. But I will always be Sammy the Bull."

Dad told me about life in the Mafia and the codes they were supposed to live by. "If there's a hundred codes, we broke ninety-nine of them," he said.

I told him about my marijuana business. He found a little humor in it and then said he was glad I was out of it. I finally confessed to him that I had been the one to get Gerard arrested for mailing the pound of weed to New York. He reprimanded me, but he understood.

Although we did talk about a lot things, the hardest thing for him to talk about was my uncle Nicky, and we didn't address the issue.

Dad told me he felt like he put his family second to his other life. But now he was ready to put his blood family before his Cosa Nostra family. I felt like I really started to understand my father's character. I realized that he was a man of honor and loyalty and that he would never double-cross someone unless he was double-crossed first. I started to feel a lot less angry after talking to him that night.

When I asked him if he regretted cooperating, he said he sometimes regretted not killing John Gotti, as he had originally wanted to do while they were in jail. But he said, "I'm not living my life with regrets because I will never be able to move forward.

"And you shouldn't live with regrets from your past, you should just look toward your future."

I felt like we had moved closer to a reconciliation that night. My father seemed to be more honest with his answers than I had anticipated. A lot had happened to me these last seven years because of his choices. I always seemed to be reacting instead of initiating things and thinking them through. I had been vacillating between being bitter about my father and wanting to forgive him and move forward. But we still had a lot more work to do.

Even though Dad had opted out of the witness protection program in Boulder, in Phoenix he was still living under the alias of Jimmy Moran. He was the highest-ranking gangster to ever break the blood oath of silence. He had gotten a lot of people sent to jail, and the ones who were still out were mad about that.

The FBI gave him as much protection as it could. They were concerned about him living his life so openly, and would check in on him from time to time. But my father refused to live his life in fear. He was already hard at work, doing the best he could to move forward. Back in his "Gambino days," a large part of his income was money he made skimming from the top and controlling the unions.

Now, in Phoenix, he had started several legitimate ventures. He had a construction company called Marathon Development, the same name as his construction company in New York. The business made nice money in home building. My father also had the pool installation company, Creative Pools, which was where he employed me. He was excavating and installing in-ground pools for people all over the Phoenix area. He seemed very excited to welcome me on board.

He had talked Mom and Gerard into selling the bagel business, which he didn't think was earning enough, and he bought a high-end restaurant in Scottsdale, fifteen miles from downtown Phoenix. My mother managed it, and my brother was the chef. Gerard had gone to culinary school in Arizona and loved to cook, so Uncle Sal's was the perfect place to show off his skills in the kitchen.

Sammy Gravano, still known as Jimmy Moran to everybody who wasn't family, was a regular. He was hardworking and well liked. It looked like everything was finally coming together for him in Phoenix. On some days, being with him brought me back to 1989, when I ran the Exotic Touch that was connected to his construction office in Brooklyn.

As time went by, my father's real name and true identity became known. In contrast to what many people in the New York community felt about my father and his decision to cooperate, people in Arizona were attracted to him, both as the real-thing New York mobster and as the country's most famous gangster to turn state's evidence. They thought it was cool to be close to us, the Gravanos.

The amount of status and respect was totally welcomed by Gerard and me, too. For a while, it gave us back the sense of reverence that we had left behind in New York. People kind of worshipped us again. Of course, this was the kind of respect that attracted the wrong types of people, but I was not conscious of this at the time. I was thrilled to be popular instead of shunned.

Dad was so proud to have me back.

Three weeks after I had settled back into life in the southwest, my brother's infant son, Nicholas, was diagnosed with spinal meningitis. Gerard and his longtime girlfriend had moved in together to raise the baby. Doctors didn't think the child would survive. He made it, but his brush with death was a turning point for me. I decided I never wanted to be so far away from my family again.

I was harboring a secret from them, however. The previous week, I had learned that I was pregnant, and Dave Seabrook was the father. I didn't want to tell anyone, not even Dave at first. At the time, I knew I was in love with him, but I had made the decision to leave him behind when I left New York. I wasn't sure myself what I was going to do about the pregnancy. I briefly thought about aborting, but I couldn't go through with it. I was in Arizona to make a fresh start, but what I quickly learned was that you can't leave the life behind.

The hardest person to tell about my pregnancy was my father. I knew he wouldn't approve. Dave had two things going against him. First, he was an ex-con. I was sure Dad would not like the fact that Dave had been in prison for robbery and attempted murder. Second, he was black and I was concerned that my father wouldn't understand that. When Dad pictured his little girl getting married, he'd had a legitimate businessman, a doctor, a lawyer, or even a construction guy in mind. Dad had been relieved when I came out to Arizona and left Lee behind, and here I was with another street guy. I remember practicing for an hour how I was going to break the news to him. Basically, nothing I had rehearsed came out when I finally sat down on the couch next to him in Mom's living room.

"I'm pregnant with a black man's baby," I blurted out.

Dad looked at me kind of in shock. "Okay, is this some random black man? Or do you know him?"

"I know him."

Dad stood up, grabbed his car keys, and left the house.

The next day I called him and asked if I could come over and talk. He said yes, so I brought Mom and Gerard with me for reinforcements. We sat down in his living room. The first words out of my mouth were, "Are you going to kill him?"

"No, but I can tell you this much, if I was still in New York, I probably would have killed him, and not because of whether he is black or white but because of the way you told me and the lack of respect I feel you have for me."

My father never taught me to judge people by color or race. He had always taught me to judge a person on his character, and I let him know that I believed that Dave was a good person. And I also felt that he would be a good man to our child.

My father was not happy that Dave was a street kid, because he wanted a better life for me. He wanted to know how he was planning to provide for me and his soon-to-be granddaughter. I told him that I was confused. That Dave would be leaving New York to come here, and that he would try to find work in Phoenix. I think Dad's disappointment was that I just came home pregnant and that he hadn't gotten a chance to know my boyfriend and the future father of my first child. But he gave me his word that he would allow Dave to come around him and welcome him into his life, if that was what I chose to do. Dad was a man of his word.

Dave flew out to Arizona to meet Dad. I was freaking out a little bit. I was worried how things were going to go.

I picked Dave up at the airport and we drove to Mom's house. Dave came in the house and my mother welcomed him. That night, my father, mother, Dave, and I went out to dinner. I was nervous that my father was meeting him and I was already pregnant. Dave seemed calm.

Dad and Dave joked about prison. Dad let Dave know that he didn't want a street guy for his daughter. He wanted to know his reason for wanting to come to Arizona, and what his intentions were in terms of making a living and supporting me and the baby.

I didn't want anything to go wrong. I had decided I really wanted the baby and I didn't want there to be any tension or bad feelings between my father and the man that I was with. The get-together went okay.

Dave moved to Arizona, rented an apartment, and found a job as a plumber. Everything seemed to be going fine. Dave even went out and bought me a ring because he knew how important being married was to Italian families. Dave went to my father to ask for my hand, and Dad said, "If you can tame her, and you can live with her for the rest of your life, then good luck, I give you my blessing."

It seemed like everything in Arizona was coming together. I had a job, Dave had a job, I had a baby on the way, Gerard and Mom were running the restaurant, and Dad was in construction. Dave proposed to me, and I said yes. But we were going to take it day by day. We knew we were having a girl, and I wanted to wait to get married until after the baby was born.

I was getting ready to move into the apartment with Dave

when Dad suggested that he move in with my mother and me to save money.

"You guys can help her with the bills. You can start looking for a place, you can put away some money, you can get your credit right, and some time in the future you can get a house," he instructed. So Dave moved in with Mom and me.

Not long after Dave got out there, my brother split up with his girlfriend again. They were on again and off again, and I worried that he didn't have any friends outside of their relationship. Gerard was still the chef at Uncle Sal's in Scottsdale. I was encouraging him to have some fun, make new friends and build a new life. But change is always hard.

Around then, my cousin Gina started dating a guy named Michael. Michael was also a chef at Uncle Sal's and a partner in the business. He was a party animal. Gina was in her late teens, but wasn't into the party scene like Michael was. She and Michael were going out to the nightclubs. I stayed behind at home; I didn't like partying pregnant. I was always tired and nauseous and just wanted to go to bed. I encouraged Dave to go out with Michael and make some friends. To help business at the restaurant, Michael started inviting lots of people he was meeting to patronize Uncle Sal's.

My father had written a book with journalist Peter Maas called *Underboss: Sammy the Bull Gravano's Story of Life in the Mafia.* Maas had also written *The Valachi Papers* and *Serpico.* The book was a sensation. Dad had been interviewed by Diane Sawyer on *Prime Time Live.* The segment, which aired on April 16, 1997, was watched by millions of people across the country. As part of the conditions of the interview, they met in a mutually agreed-upon setting far from Phoenix. Sawyer protected Dad's whereabouts. She put it like this: *"We should point out we do not know where Gravano lives. We agreed to meet him at an inn in a remote valley in California.*

"But as you'll see, amazingly, he's not in disguise. He says he's prudent, but he's not the kind of guy who lives in fear." So, Dad's face was out there.

The *Prime Time* interview caught the attention of a local reporter from the *Arizona Republic,* Dennis Wagner, who did a little digging and learned that Gerard Gravano had been arrested on drug charges in Phoenix the year before. The arrest had been when Gerard had tried to mail me the pound of marijuana.

After a little more nosing around, Wagner found out that Sammy the Bull was also in Phoenix. With the national attention my father got from being on Diane Sawyer, and having a bestselling book, Wagner knew he had a hot scoop when he found Dad.

The FBI tried to stop the newspaper from publishing Wagner's story. Even though my father had signed himself out of witness protection, they tried to offer him the best protection they could. The agents most familiar with him even stopped by to hang out if they were in the Phoenix area. Dad wasn't too happy when the reporter started showing up at the restaurant and at Dad's construction office; he even started calling my mother's house trying to speak to any one of us. Dad agreed that it was better to give Wagner the story and just meet with him so that he would go away.

Against the objections of the FBI, the *Arizona Republic* printed the article with the headline "SAMMY THE BULL SURFACES IN THE VALLEY OF THE SUN." My father was still good at being a cover story; that much was for sure.

When the article was published and everyone in the Phoenix area learned who Jimmy Moran was, my father's businesses suffered. At first, Dad's customers at the pool business were nervous to patronize him, so things slowed down there. But nervousness came with a certain amount of intrigue and the restaurant became more popular. People fascinated by us starting coming into Uncle Sal's to catch a glimpse of one of us. Unfortunately, some of them were the wrong kind of people, drug dealers, petty thugs, and those who looked up to that kind of lifestyle. The FBI was very concerned about that. My father was not supposed to hang out with the criminal element, and he stopped coming around.

"I'm going to lay low for a while," he told us. "I'm just going to do my construction, go to the gym, and go home at night." However, he loved Gerard's cooking. He couldn't pass up a good meal. He would sneak into the restaurant, pick up takeout, and sneak back out. He was in the background stopping by on his way home, in and out to pick up his food.

Meanwhile, Gerard and I were soaking up the attention. It felt good to be back on top. We were making all these new friends, mostly tough guys who frequented the nightclubs and were involved in dealing drugs. Arizona, like New York and every other place in the world, was an active market for illegal drugs. Ecstasy was the up-and-coming high, all the local nightclubs were flooded with it. It only made sense that local drug dealers would search out and befriend my brother, a real Gravano.

One of the local dealers was a college kid, a former New Yorker by the name of Mike Papa. I met him for the first time on New Year's Eve 1999. He came across as very studious. He was going to Arizona State University, and taking pre-med classes. He loved hanging around with Gerard, almost like a stalker.

His brother had gotten in trouble and needed a lawyer, and so Gerard referred him to the attorney that Gerard had used for his marijuana case. The lawyer was having dinner with my father at Uncle Sal's one night. Dad said he had a client for him, Gerard's friend. Mike came to the restaurant to introduce himself and to thank my father for getting him the lawyer. He brought Dad a box of cigars.

Mike was really intrigued with my father. He had even read his book, *Underboss*. Maybe Mike thought being around the family of a famous mobster made him important. I'd seen my share of these guys in New York. You could tell they were trying to get something.

Dad was flattered that Mike had read his book and that he held him in such high regard. He was really happy that Mike had befriended Gerard. Mike was a university student and a fellow New Yorker, and Dad was impressed with both of these credentials. Dad didn't know that Mike Papa was a drug dealer, and Gerard and I didn't tell him.

Mike started hanging around my father. He was an extremely well-educated guy, and Dad thought he could be an asset to his pool company. Dad was going to let him become the head sales guy. Mike was good-looking and charming. Pools were getting sold when he came on board and business was improving.

Unbeknownst to anyone, Mike was telling people that he was rolling with Sammy the Bull, and he was partners with him and his son. At the time, my father had no idea that Mike was going around using his name, nor did he know that he was under surveillance by the police for being a suspected drug dealer.

In the nightclubs, we knew Mike as a celebrity kid. Everybody seemed to want to be around him. We didn't know how much trouble he was in until much later. Gerard and I both knew that Mike dabbled in drug dealing, but we had no idea how long he'd been doing it or what the extent of his involvement was. Members of the Gilbert Police Department had him under surveillance even before he met Gerard. The code name for the investigation was the "Papa Organization."

Gerard and I also had no idea that he was a member of a gang in Gilbert, Arizona. We knew that his brother Kevin belonged to a white supremacist group called the Devil Dogs, so named because members barked as they assaulted victims. Kevin had been arrested and the story was all over the news. That's why Mike had needed the name of a lawyer. But he insisted that he was nothing like his brother and painted a picture of himself as a dedicated pre-med student. Normally, when somebody first met my father, they tried to impress him with their street credentials, but Mike did the opposite. He tried to make Dad believe that his ambition was to become a doctor.

Dad had no idea that Mike had asked Gerard if he knew where he could get Ecstasy. Mike thought my brother could hook up a deal. Gerard knew people in New York, and Mike threw my brother money for hooking him up. I started to worry that something bad was going to happen to Gerard.

All his life, Mom and Dad had tried to protect Gerard. When kids snubbed him on Todt Hill, we moved. If he wasn't doing well in school, Dad hired tutors. When he was diagnosed with dyslexia, Dad took him to every specialist in New York he could find. When Mom left Staten Island, she brought Gerard with her. And now here was this punk Mike Papa using my brother for leverage in drug dealing.

My father always wanted my brother to be a legitimate kid.

He never felt Gerard was cut out for the street life. Even in Phoenix, Dad's biggest fear was that someone from New York who wanted to make a name for himself would try to kill my brother, now that he wasn't a kid anymore. But as a parent, he only had so much control over his kids' actions and choices.

The whole thing was like a perfect storm. Gerard was spending more and more time with his new buddies at the restaurant. He knew what they were up to, and got involved in dealing willingly, nobody made him do it. He was only working with Mike, though. He never went out and pedaled pills. It was Mike doing the dealing, and Gerard just lent him some money. These guys were seeing that they were getting more respect hanging around with my brother. That Mike was intrigued by the Gravanos struck me as weird, but I went with it. I didn't try and stop it.

But when they started talking about going to New York, I got nervous. My brother had been doing some pretty irresponsible things before his new friends came on the scene. He was living beyond his means, buying things he couldn't afford, and getting himself into debt. He decided he could participate in a couple of drug transactions to get himself in the clear. I tried to tell Gerard not to go to New York with money, but he wouldn't listen. He was planning to hook up with some of his old contacts and make a deal big enough to erase his outstanding debt.

There had already been a hit out on his life once, two years after Dad had cooperated. There was no one left in New York to protect us. Lee had done it until he found out I was with Dave. Whether it was because I was with a new guy or because Dave was black, Lee didn't like that I was with Dave, and he was no longer going to protect either me or Gerard.

I was in a mess. My brother and I were trained to never

tattle on each other. We'd get punished by my father if we did. But I was scared for Gerard's life. I was compelled to go to my father and tell him what was going on.

Dad flipped when I told him Gerard's plan. "Get in the car," he demanded to me. He drove straight to my brother's house, kicked in the front door, and put a gun to Gerard's head. "I'll help you kill yourself!" he screamed. "Here's the gun!"

Dad was furious. "We have so much to offer," he yelled, pressing the nozzle against my brother's temple. "We are finally winning. We are finally getting ahead." He was beside himself.

"Dad, it's only a couple of times," Gerard pleaded.

"I don't give a shit!" my father screamed.

Looking back, I wish I had never told my father because then he wouldn't have been forced to get involved. Things always get complicated when you try to fix somebody else's problems, I learned.

After the blowup at Gerard's apartment, the three of us went out to dinner. Dad was still upset. "I feel like after I cooperated, every decision you and your brother have made has been to spite me," he said to us. "We lost everything we had. We need to see the big picture when we make decisions."

Everybody in the family was confused about what mattered: respect, money, forgiveness, family. So much had happened to us that we hadn't talked about. We were all going through the process of forgiving each other.

Dad had given Gerard everything money could buy. He had bought him his own restaurant. He had given him the down payment on a house. He was at a loss as to why Gerard would want to take such a risk going to New York to do a drug deal. To me it was clear, Gerard wanted respect more than money.

Dad's resolution was to lend my brother money so he

wouldn't have to go back to New York to do the drug deal. Dad felt he was protecting him from the possibility of being harmed in New York because he was involved in some criminal activity.

Gerard promised my father that he would stop dealing, but he and Mike never really stopped. There were a few more deals. There was this kid named Jason who was a rival seller. Mike and Gerard ended up beating him up outside of a nightclub and leaving him there. They didn't know Jason was connected to an Israeli crime outfit out of New York, which was transporting a lot of Ecstasy from New York to Los Angeles and Arizona.

The assault on Jason got the Israeli mob really mad. Mike Papa came to the pool office and told my dad that Israeli mobsters found out that he, Sammy the Bull, was in Phoenix and they were going to have him taken down. They were going to kill him and Gerard. Mike told Dad there had been a fight and he and Gerard had beaten up the kid. But he failed to tell both Gerard and my father about his side of the drug dealings and the personal beef that he had with this kid Jason.

Dad told Mike, "Get me a meeting at Uncle Sal's."

Dad had no idea what it was about. Jason showed up at the restaurant for the meeting. "I'm telling you right now, if anything happens to my son, there is going to be an all-out war," my father told the guy.

"We own Arizona," the Israeli guy replied.

"No," Dad said. "I own Arizona. Tell your boss that Sammy the Bull is here, and he owns Arizona now."

My daughter Karina took two days to be born. I was living at my mother's, and Dave had just moved into the house. Karina's due date was June 26, 1999, but she wasn't born until July 7. My doctor let me go two weeks past my due date, but then he was going to induce me if she hadn't come by then. On July 5, I went to Desert Samaritan Hospital in Mesa to deliver. Everybody came to the hospital: Mom, Gerard, Aunt Diane, Dad, even Grandma Scibetta, who arrived from Florida to be with me for the birth. I was put on Pitocin, but I was not dilating. So I was going to be allowed to sleep through the night, and they were going to try again the next day. But nothing happened. I was having contractions, but not dilating. I was right next to the labor room and I was going crazy hearing all the new mothers going in and out and having their babies. I begged for a C-section, telling the doctor I'd already been there two days.

The whole day of July 6 went by, and now it was the morning of July 7. I got up to take a shower and pack my things. The nurse saw me walking around the room and asked what was going on. "I'm going to another hospital that will help me have my baby," I told her. She disappeared into the hallway and returned with the doctor.

"I give you my word, you are going to have the baby tonight," he assured me.

I didn't trust him, so I called my father. I reached him at the construction office. "Dad, can you come down here, and if I don't have the baby tonight, can you do something?" I begged him. He promised he'd make it happen, but not before teasing me.

"Karen," he said, "you're like a little bull. The baby doesn't want to come." I was ready to kill him.

At 5:00 P.M., I was still not dilating. Just as they were thinking about prepping me for a C-section, I started dilating. Within an hour I was fully dilated. Finally, Karina was delivered, weighing in at six pounds, seven ounces.

Unfortunately, Karina had an irregular heartbeat when she was born, so she had to be raced to the NICU before I even had a chance to see her. My brother had been waiting in the hall, and when he saw all the commotion as the team wrapped her and ran her along in her isolette, he busted into the delivery room, where my legs were still in stirrups.

"Are you okay?" he asked in a panic.

"I'm okay," I told him.

Everybody except my mother and grandmother went up to the NICU to get updates. The team was really scared about Karina's low heart rate. She was such a fighter, though. She was soon out of the NICU and in my arms. Instantly, she was the love of my life. It was such a crazy feeling realizing I'd made a baby. My perspective changed after that. Once you have a child, you have to be the caregiver. From that moment on, I didn't want to be in trouble. I wanted to be a perfect mother.

When we got home, Dave didn't know what to do with her. My little crying baby, she would cry all the time. I'd feel guilty that I was doing things wrong, but she was full of colic. Every time she would start to cry, Dave would hand her back to me. My father called her his little peanut, but he'd hand her back to me, too, if she started to wail.

Dave and I prepared a nursery in one of the bedrooms of Mom's house. I decorated it in pink and propped a giant pink stuffed bunny in one corner. But we rarely used the room, since it was on the other side of the house from our bedroom. Instead, we set up a bassinet and Karina stayed with us.

I started working for my father at the pool company a couple of weeks after Karina was born. Although I was happy as an aesthetician, I felt that having a newborn I needed a job with more flexible hours. Dad had an office in the back where I could feed and change the baby, so it made more sense.

I was excited to be working with Dad. We were beginning to build up the pool company. We were adding a pool cleaning service that Gerard and Dave were going to run. Dad's excavation company dug the pools, the pool company installed them, and the pool cleaning service offered monthly contracts to our customers. Being at the pool company meant I would be dealing with Jen, the assistant my father felt so proud of, who I found condescending, competitive, and cold. She had grown up without a father, and made me feel unappreciative of mine. It was okay, though. I was overjoyed to be working with Dad. It was funny, all the resentment just left after I had Karina. I came to realize that your child is the most important thing of all. My father had done the best he could for all of us under the circumstances, and I was going to do my best for Karina. Crime was not going to be the way.

None of us had any idea that the Phoenix police were watching Dad's construction company. He had been under constant surveillance.

Someone gave the Phoenix police a tip that Mike Papa was hooked up with the Italian Mafia, and said there was some big guy from the Italian Mafia in Phoenix. They found out Mike was friends with Gerard Gravano, and that Mike was investing in a pool company that was owned by Debra Gravano and a restaurant that was owned by Mom, Gerard, and Gina's boyfriend, Mike.

The cops put surveillance on Gerard and Mike Papa. They were hanging out in the nightclubs and the cops started asking, "Who are these kids hanging out with Mike Papa?" They saw Gerard. They saw Mike reporting to Marathon Development, which was also in the name of Debra Gravano. Now they said, "Wait a minute, is this Sammy the Bull?" The Phoenix police marked their investigation as top secret, and didn't tell the FBI what they were up to because they feared the agents would uproot Dad.

They wiretapped all of our phones, and they put a bug under Dad's desk in the construction office. Dad knew about the Ecstasy, it was supposed to be over. As far as the police were concerned, they saw this organization and that everybody was answering to this "big guy," because everyone on the cell phones was using Dad's name to gain respect in the streets. In one conversation, Mike Papa was talking to a guy he had shorted ten thousand dollars.

The drug source called Mike up and said, "The money you gave me is short ten thousand dollars."

"My Godfather gave it to me and he counted it himself," had been Mike's response, which police recorded.

My father had lent Gerard and Mike money. The loan was supposed to be a onetime thing to pull Gerard out of the drug business. The cops had all our phones bugged, so they heard the conversations.

Mike was throwing around Dad's name for credibility, and in this case, to get himself out of a bind. The guy was a thug, and he was trying to shield himself behind Dad and further his street credibility by using my father's name and his connection to Gerard.

At the same time as Dad learned about the supposed hit from the Israeli mob, John Gotti's brother, Peter, had a hit team coming down to Phoenix to find my father. The FBI told Dad they had reason to believe there was a hit team in the area looking for him. My father thought he was already in conversation with the guy who the FBI was talking about, the Israeli mobster from the restaurant.

Dad called Mike Papa, "I don't know what you're doing," he lit into him. "I lent you money."

Two days later, we all got arrested for being a drug cartel.

CHAPTER EIGHTEEN

"Karen, come out with your hands up!"

A number of events led up to the fateful morning when my entire family was taken into custody. The Mafia hit team, which included Thomas "Huck" Cabonaro and a guy named Fat Sal, were in Phoenix surveying my father's construction office. At the same time, the Phoenix police were also watching the office. The FBI was coming to Arizona to talk to Dad about testifying in another Mafia case. The Israeli mobsters were threatening Gerard, Mike Papa, and Dad. And Mike was running the Ecstasy ring behind my father's back.

Early on the morning of February 24, 2000, I'd gotten out of bed to feed Karina. She was seven months old and prone to colic. I was trying to get her to settle back down with a bottle in the nursery when I heard people talking outside the window.

"Move the fuck over," a male voice demanded.

When I moved the curtains over, I saw a person in a black mask staring at me from the other side of the window. I didn't know if someone wanted to rob the house or kill us. I was in complete shock.

A few seconds later, a voice at the front door shouted, "Open the fucking door." At that moment, the door flew off its hinges and armed men in black masks began filing into the house. They grabbed my mother and threw her down on the ground. Glass was shattering everywhere. I didn't know what was happening.

Dave came running out of the bedroom. Just when I was about to run after him, I remembered the baby was in the bassinet in my bedroom, so I ran back in and locked the door. The intruders were wearing tactical helmets that had lights shining from them so they could see in the dark. They were throwing smoke bombs into the rooms and the air was thick and black.

I picked up Karina, wrapped her in a blanket, and placed her in the closet.

"Karen, come out with your hands up," came the husky voice from the hallway. They obviously knew who I was since they were addressing me by name.

"I have a baby," I shouted back, taking Karina back into my arms.

"Open the fucking door!"

"No, I have my daughter, and she is sick," I screamed. I didn't know who the intruders were, but they sure as hell weren't going to hurt my baby. "She has pinkeye," I yelled, hoping somebody sympathetic would intervene.

I could hear my mother yelling from the other room. "Please, please. She's sick."

I finally opened the door and was immediately confronted by a masked person holding a gun. *"Police!"* he screamed with an apparent adrenaline surge. "Give me the baby!" He tried to snatch my daughter from my arms. I could feel Karina's tiny fingers clinging to my shirt, pinching at my skin.

Maybe he thought I was armed, the way he was behaving. "You have two options," I said firmly. "You're either going to take me out with my baby or in a body bag, but either way, I'm holding the baby!"

"Let her hold the baby!" My mother was screaming from down on the floor, where she was being handcuffed. I had no idea why the cops were behaving like this or what they wanted with us. I figured it had something to do with my brother. I was just hoping they didn't find him. Gerard was supposed to be coming by any minute to drop off Nicholas on his way to work.

Our arrests were right out of an action film, way more terrifying if you are on the receiving end of the tactical takedown. I later learned that Phoenix police and DEA (Drug Enforcement Agency) agents had hit about fifteen houses simultaneously. People under suspicion of being drug dealers were being arrested all across town in a sting that had been in the making for more than a year. My father's had been the first one on the list of suspects they were taking in. He was the big prize.

I didn't know it at the time, but my brother was in the neighborhood when the cops busted into our house. When he'd pulled onto our street, he saw that the entire house was surrounded and roped off. There were about fifteen cop cars parked in front of the house, and helicopters were hovering overheard.

He circled the block a couple of times, frantically dialing

Dad. When he couldn't reach him, he called cousin Gina. Gina and my aunt raced to our house to get Karina and bring her to their house. The agents kept my mother and me sitting in handcuffs on the couch for forty-five minutes waiting for them.

Gerard drove to Dad's house, but it had been roped off, too. When both our houses were being busted, he figured a sting was going down, so he took off to find a place to get his head together. He couldn't help any of us, but he turned himself in a couple of hours after we were taken into custody when he knew there was a warrant out for his arrest as well.

Mom and I were among forty-five people arrested that morning. We were taken in a squad car to police headquarters in Phoenix and thrown in a cell with about thirty other law-breakers, prostitutes, and drug addicts, and there was no-where to sit.

"Can she sit down?" I asked a younger person, who had a place.

"She can sit down, but she needs to give me her food," the lady said.

Mom resisted. She had been given a pack containing a prison lunch.

"Ma, what do you want? You're not gonna eat this, just give her the food," I told her. Besides, the food from the prison kitchen was coming in another hour.

I knew we were being linked to Mike Papa's Ecstasy ring, but I wasn't sure how Mom and I fit in. We were selected to be taken to a different part of the precinct for processing, special treatment of the wrong kind. I'd overhead officers saying we were part of the "upper echelon" of the "operation."

One of our new cellmates asked my mother what we were in

for. "I don't know. They're saying I am a bankroller to a big drug syndicate," Mom answered.

"Mrs. G., do you think I can get a job when we get out?" she wanted to know, addressing her like an old friend. You can't make this shit up. Like I said, the celebrity and the life followed all of us wherever we went.

I figured out that we were probably under arrest for selling Ecstasy. But it didn't make sense. There were so many cop cars, helicopters, and agents with masks, complete overkill for the situation. It was only a couple of drug transactions.

I was also wondering about my father. I knew he had guns, and I worried what he might do. He later told me he'd woken up to the sound of his dog Petie barking and had already hit the floor.

Dad was always on alert. To me, it seemed he must have been on alert since the day he was born. Once, when we were at a movie theater in Phoenix, he pulled a gun from his pocket and was poised to use it on a guy who seemed to be following us. I didn't know what was happening. We were just leaving the movie theater when he had grabbed me by the arm and ordered me to keep walking. I watched in horror as he put his hand on the revolver stuck in the back of his pants. The movie patron stalking us turned out to be a guy who recognized Sammy the Bull and wanted my father to autograph Dad's book, *Underboss*, which he was holding behind his back. Dad had mistaken the book for a gun and was ready to react. The request was resolved amicably, thank God.

The morning of the sting, the cops got to my dad before he could get his gun. He was crawling for it, but the place was stormed so fast he couldn't reach it. He thought they were hit men. If it was a hit team, Dad was going to go out with a fight.

Dad was a convicted felon so he wasn't supposed to have a gun, but he always felt he needed one in case anything was to go down.

Dad was brought to the same jail as us, but was being held in a different area, so we were completely in the dark about what was going on with him. My mother and I were released on bail the next day. My brother had turned himself in and it took a couple of days before my grandparents could come up with the money to post bail. All of our assets had been frozen, so Gerard had to wait until my grandparents could put up their house for bail. My father was held at the jail in downtown Phoenix, in solitary confinement. His bail was set at five million dollars cash, impossible to make, especially since they had frozen all of our assets.

Pretty much from that day on, it was like drama. The cops wanted to make an example of my father. They confiscated our homes, boats, and businesses. They told the court that my father was the mastermind of an Ecstasy drug ring, and we in his family each played a role. They were claiming that Dad's ring was distributing twenty-five thousand Ecstasy pills a week, selling them for twenty-five dollars a tablet to teenagers in the area. Dad and Gerard were also charged with the same crimes in New York, since they were supposedly dealing between New York and Arizona. The charges simply weren't true. But "the life" follows you wherever you go.

Gerard's friend Mike Papa was also arrested and charged as a member of the ring, which police were now calling the Sammy the Bull Organization.

When the Gilbert police turned the case over to the Phoenix police, they had been investigating Mike Papa for years. They considered him the drug ring's leader and called the ring the Mike Papa Organization. They knew that Gerard had only been a friend of Mike Papa for a short time. But once the investigation was in the hands of the police in Phoenix, suddenly my father was the main target, even though he hadn't even been on the radar before that. Dad was considered a big fish, so cracking a case that involved Sammy Gravano, even if the charges were trumped up, could be career making. Once in the hands of the Phoenix police the name of the drug organization suddenly changed from the Mike Papa Organization to the Sammy the Bull Organization.

Dave had been in on a couple of deals with Gerard and Mike Papa, so he was arrested, too. Because police had seen him entering the house and knew that he lived with Debra Gravano, they claimed that Dave was the runner and that he was storing the drugs in the house, which had now become the ring's "headquarters."

This wasn't the end of the story, as with all good Mafia stories, this one had a twist. Turned out that top members of the Gambino family were planning a hit on Dad. Dad's interview in *Vanity Fair* magazine had put Peter Gotti in a position where he felt he needed to react on my father. In the article, Dad had said he wasn't afraid of anybody in the Gambino crime family. Peter Gotti, acting capo, sanctioned a hit. He recruited my uncle Eddie to plan it and Huck and Fat Sal to come to Arizona to carry it out.

They had been in Phoenix, casing out Dad's construction office and apartment. Huck had taken on a disguise as a gruffy, bearded Hells Angel biker. The two men were considering a sniper attack or a car bomb. They opted for the bomb, because they felt it would be easier and they wouldn't have to get too close to my father. Knowing Sammy, they feared that he might win. It was scary to think that Gerard, Nicholas, Mom, Karina, or I could have been in that car with my father when it exploded. The hit never went off because Dad was taken into custody.

A short time after that, Fat Sal cooperated with the Feds and testified in a case where all three men, Peter, Huck, and Uncle Eddie, were charged with attempted murder and sentenced to prison.

Life in Phoenix was now hard for all of us. I was thankful I was only on probation, but soon Mom, Karina, and I were going to have no place to live, no place to work, and no money. The Feds had frozen all of our assets. They said everything we owned had been bought with drug money. Even though much of our property had been brought to Arizona from Staten Island long before any involvement with drug dealing, they confiscated it anyway. Our bank accounts and credit cards were frozen, so we had no access to cash or credit.

I was distraught. "Oh my God," I said to myself. "What am I going to do about my seven-month-old daughter? How am I going to be able to take care of this child? What is going to happen to Karina and Nicolas?"

The Attorney General's Office was forcing Mom to put the house on Secretariat Drive on the market and they were going to keep all the proceeds from that sale, as well. We had a couple of months to get packed and vacate, so there was a lot of chaos. Gerard was out on bail, awaiting sentencing. But Dad was stuck in jail until he was sentenced. I was really stressed.

One crazy June day, I was the only one home with the two kids. There was a huge pool in the backyard. The property was surrounded by a six-foot fence, but there was no fence around the pool. However, every door in the house had locks very high up. Mom had a pit bull named Keisha and he had a way of opening the screen door if he needed to get out. I was playing a game with Nicholas, who wasn't even two at the time. I'd hide a little toy and he would try to find it and bring it back to me.

The phone rang and I took the call for just a couple of minutes. I assumed Nicholas was in pursuit of the toy. But he wasn't coming back. I noticed the dog was outside, and realized that the screen door he pushed open to get there had not reclosed entirely. I ran outside and down to the pool. Nicholas was at the bottom of the pool, not moving. I jumped in and pulled his lifeless body out. He was blue and not breathing. I didn't know how to do CPR. I dialed 911. I was hysterical and the 911 operator managed to calm me down to talk me through it.

"You need to listen to me so I can help you," he told me. I was freaking out. It was the worst experience of my life. After the 911 operator brought me into focus, it became a completely out of body experience. I did CPR just as he told me to. Mom pulled into the driveway from grocery shopping just as the paramedics arrived.

The doorbell rang and I ran to answer it. It was the cop who had been coming by Gerard's house to make sure he was obeying his curfew. "Oh my God, please tell me it's not Nicholas," he cried. The officer called Gerard at the restaurant and told him to come to his mother's house. There had been an accident.

When my brother got there, I couldn't even look at him. "I almost killed your kid," I cried. "I am so sorry, I almost killed your son."

Nicholas was put in an ambulance bound for Desert Samaritan Hospital. I was taken to a trauma shock unit at the same hospital. My father was in jail when the story of Nicholas's near drowning ran on the news that evening. A correction's officer came to find Dad in his cell.

"Sammy, I think you need to call home," he told him. "Something just happened at your house."

Dad was calling the house, but no one was answering. A guy from the restaurant ended up driving over to the jail to deliver a message. "Tell Sammy that everyone is okay."

I was horrified that my 911 call with the dispatcher had been played on the news that evening. I don't ever want to listen to that phone call. To this day, I can still feel the overwhelming horror that overcame me when I realized that Nicholas had gotten out of my sight.

In Arizona, drowning deaths are so common, and we owned a pool company. You think you can just turn away for two seconds. I thought Nicholas was in the house. The doctor at the hospital determined that he was only under water for two minutes when I found him. The dog must have run through the screen, and Nicholas probably went to throw the toy in the pool. He had a scratch on his chin that we believe he got when he fell in. Every day, I thank God that he is alive.

CHAPTER NINETEEN

"Don't lie now, you are under oath."

On the day of the plea, June 29, 2001, Mom and I arrived at the Maricopa County Superior Court together. We didn't know when Gerard and Dad were getting there. They were coming straight from the jail because my father hadn't been able to make bail. We weren't allowed to see them before the proceedings.

That day in court was the first time I had laid eyes on the plea. It was a universal plea, so we all had to admit that we were part of a criminal organization run by my father, that Dad was the mastermind. Then we all had to plead guilty to the charges attributed to each of us or the deal was off and they were going to put it all on Gerard.

I was pleading guilty "to illegal use of an electronic

communication device." I didn't even know what that meant. My lawyer told me it meant that I had used a telephone to discuss a drug transaction. "I am not signing this plea," I told him. I didn't want to be a party to my father and brother going to prison. "What are my consequences if I go to trial?"

"Pretty much probation," the lawyer told me.

"I am going to get probation anyway," I said. "So take me to trial."

"Karen, we discussed this with your father, and you are going to sign it."

I had this sick-to-my-stomach feeling. I didn't want to sign the plea. It was ridiculous to me. "Where is my father?" I demanded.

I was informed that Dad and Gerard were in the back, in two different holding cells.

"Can I see them?" I inquired. The answer was no.

The courtroom was packed. I knew it was going to be based on the prior court hearings. Everybody, especially the media, wanted to see Sammy the Bull. My mother, sitting beside me, was a nervous wreck, too. Judge Steven Sheldon hadn't taken the bench yet, but I had to sign the plea before the proceedings could begin anyway.

I had a very nervous feeling. I didn't want to do this. I knew that my father could get up to twenty years. I just wanted to stand up and say, "They are fucking lying. It didn't happen this way. Let me get five years and let him get less time."

I knew my father didn't start the organization, and he didn't do what they were accusing him of. He lent the money trying to help out. He didn't want us in this lifestyle.

I'd lied to him. I hadn't told tell him that Mike Papa was a drug dealer when I first met him. I got scared when Gerard said he was going to go back to New York. I always feared that he could get robbed or something could happen to him.

I had been the one to tell my father and get him involved. The fact that Gerard had already had one serious threat against him already made everybody do things they wouldn't have otherwise done. At that point, Dad was trying to rebuild a relationship with his kids. To warn us, "Don't do this," wasn't going to work.

Two months later, the entire Phoenix police force was kicking in our doors and putting it all on my father. Once the media got ahold of it, the headlines were out there, blaring our guilt.

I felt bad, like what the fuck did I do? Here I fought this man, I tested him, I hid the truth from him, which normally I would never have done, but I'd lost respect for him. Now, here he was going to take twenty years in prison to protect his son, and nothing was going to happen to me. The pleas that we signed were worded very strategically.

Dad's last one had been a sweetheart deal. He'd killed nineteen people and he had only served five years. It felt as though the authorities were trying to rectify that deal.

Gerard and I had given the authorities this path to get to my father and I felt really bad. At that point, I felt like it was all Gerard's and my fault, and I wanted to get up in the courtroom and say my father didn't do anything. It was like he was on trial for the nineteen murders, like it was payback. But now they could say Mr. Gravano sold drugs.

I already didn't like the government because I felt my father had joined forces with them and now they were turning on him. Look what you did for them, and here they are.

I heard a lot of commotion when the side door of the courtroom opened. A couple of deputies were escorting my father in in shackles. He held his head high, and gave me a smile. He was always strong for all of us. This time was no exception. Gerard was brought in next, shackled like Dad. He took the seat on Dad's far side.

The first person called to step forward was me.

"Can you state your name for the record," Judge Sheldon asked me.

I couldn't even say it. I just stood there.

My lawyer next to me urged me on. "Say it, Karen, just say it," he said.

"Miss, can you state your name?" the judge repeated.

"Karen Gravano," I said in a hushed tone.

"Can you state your age?"

I was so upset I couldn't remember how old I was, and I looked back at my mother. She mouthed the number twenty-nine for me.

Dad spoke out and said, "Don't lie now, you are under oath." Everyone in the courtroom laughed, even the judge.

Everything was a blur after that. Mom, Dad, and Gerard each took their turns in front of the judge. It was probably one of the worst days of my life. For the first time, I was standing there and I was like what did I do? How did this happen? How did we get here?

We each signed our plea and were instructed to return to the same courtroom on September 28, for sentencing. I had pled guilty to "use of wire or electronic communications" and "drug-related transactions." I was sentenced to three years probation. Mom got five years probation for "illegally conducting an enterprise," short for what the authorities considered her bankrolling of the whole operation. Gerard was sentenced to nine and half years in prison for "illegally conducting an enterprise" and "offering to sell and transport dangerous drugs." His sentence was a half year longer than what Dad had agreed to in the plea deal.

My father pled guilty to ten counts, including "conspiracy to sell dangerous drugs," "participating in a criminal syndicate," and "money laundering." When he went up before the bench, Judge Sheldon sentenced him to nineteen years in prison, with no possibility of early release. Dad's nineteen years meant he wouldn't be out until he was seventy-four. The sentence was longer than Dad had agreed to.

My father always maintained that the charges against him had been jacked up. A couple of years after Dad was sentenced, a police officer who was involved in the case from the very beginning came forward with information that would have been crucial to my father's defense but that we never learned about at the time.

Specifically, the officer claimed that there were transcriptions of recordings from a bug that had been planted under my father's desk. Those transcripts would have shown that my father had been trying to deter Gerard and Mike from getting into drugs and to push them more into legitimate businesses.

If this officer is correct, then the prosecution testimony that the recordings could not be transcribed was, in fact, incorrect, whether or not the witnesses who testified were aware of that fact. We also heard that prosecutors from the Eastern District of New York had urged the police to tone down Mike Papa's involvement in the drug organization so that he didn't appear as the leader.

Dad and Gerard were also brought to New York to face

federal drug-related charges because of the alleged connection with the Israeli mob, claiming the ring was in fact an interstate organization. We believe that when Mike Papa took the stand in New York against my father, he played down his role in the drug ring and prosecutors, perhaps in their zeal to get Sammy the Bull, looked the other way. This testimony is what ultimately resulted in both Dad and Gerard getting longer sentences.

My fiancé, Dave, was sentenced to nine and half years for selling drugs. Because he had violent prior convictions, he was eligible for the maximum allowable sentence under the law. He served his sentence in various prisons throughout the state of Arizona and was released in September 2010.

Mike Papa cooperated with authorities, but the amount of jail time he received was never disclosed. He is now in the witness protection program.

All of our assets were frozen and the families of Dad's victims filed wrongful death lawsuits against my father. Now that my father had violated parole, all of the protections he had received under his original plea deal with the Feds were null and void. Everybody came after us with a vengeance.

We weren't allowed to touch any of our money. Things were really tough. Mom and I helped Gerard's girlfriend to raise Nicholas, so it was like we had two babies to care for, mine and my brother's. I was angry. I felt like I was a complete victim.

I had to pay for the lawyers and take care of the family, so I kicked into gear and began hustling. My father was always a hustler, and if nothing else, he taught me to hustle. I had to take care of Karina the best I could. I was determined to make it work honestly. When I was in the jail cell with Mom that day, it had hit me hard that I had someone else beside myself to care for.

I figured I'd try to do something in facials, and started going to the day spas in the area to see if anybody was hiring. Finally, three months after I had been arrested, I got an interview. I told the lady up-front about who I was.

I said, "I'm Karen Gravano, and I am trying to get my life back. I am a licensed aesthetician and I need to provide for my family. But I'm not going to go through the interview if you are going to judge me."

The spa owner liked the way I was so honest with her, and she thought someone like me would be an asset to her. After she hired me, neither one of us told our clients who I was. We didn't think it was anybody's business. If somebody asked, I didn't lie, but it didn't come up very often. In order to hustle up my business, I handed out flyers for free facials. I was trying to get my own clientele. I was starting from scratch. I didn't have anybody. I was also building a relationship with the lady who owned the spa. After a while, I built up a big following. Word was out there that I was giving the best facials in Mesa.

I worked at the spa in the daytime, and I also worked doing makeup at a strip club at night. I was in complete "do it" mode.

My mother sold the house on Secretariat Drive, and the government took all the money. Mom, Karina, and I then moved to a smaller house not far from my aunt Diane in Tempe. My grandmother offered to give Mom a loan for the down payment.

Nicholas's mother, Mallory, was also working full-time, so she'd drop the baby at the house and either Mom or I would watch both children at the same time. The kids were fourteen months apart, and over time, they grew inseparable. While Mallory and I didn't get along at first, she understood how family-oriented Mom and I were, and she allowed us to visit with Nicholas on a regular basis. In turn, she invited Karina along on weekends when she and Nicholas were going to be doing something fun.

A year passed before I was able to take a good, deep look at myself. I needed to figure out who Karen Gravano was, besides Sammy the Bull's daughter. I also needed to figure out what my role had been to get to this point.

Dad had assured us he was taking the deal without resentment because it was best for the family. But he was still very angry and holding a grudge. He was devastated that his entire family had been brought into the fray. I had never seen my father stressed out in any case, but this was his family.

"If you'd just listened me," he'd rant. He'd go through this tirade of mixed emotions, and I was feeling a lot of guilt.

For the first five years of his incarceration, he was held in protective solitary confinement at ADX, the super-max facility in Colorado. Mom visited him there once, but because my father didn't like the conditions in which we had to see him living, none of us ever visited him there again. Dad wrote to me, though, and I'd write back.

I continued to work at the day spa in Phoenix and was raising Karina and Nicholas the best I could. I was in New York for a visit with friends in the fall of 2004 when I learned that my father was being transferred from ADX to the Metropolitan Correctional Center, where he had been so many years ago with John Gotti.

Now he was answering to the 1980 murder of New York City police officer named Peter Calabro of Saddlebrook, New Jersey. A man by the name of Richard Kuklinski, nicknamed the Iceman, had been arrested and charged in five homicides. Kuklinski was a contract killer who was believed to be responsible for more than two hundred murders.

During his confession to police, Kuklinski implicated my father in Calabro's murder. He said my dad had hired him to kill Calabro, and had even supplied the murder weapon, a gun. The whole thing was preposterous; my father had his own hit team. Why would he hire somebody? There was also no motive for the crime. It didn't even look like a Mafia-style hit. Nevertheless, prosecutors were going after my father, and he was housed in New York at the time that I was in Manhattan visiting.

I nearly keeled over when they brought Dad into the visiting area. He had been diagnosed with Graves' disease while in prison and looked near death. He was white as a ghost, and was missing teeth. The visit started out okay. He told me how much he loved me and missed me, and asked about the kids. It wasn't long before he started ripping into me. He was still so angry and said the most hurtful things, blaming me for his current inmate status because I had refused to grow up.

He complained about how I'd fought him on all his good advice to make friends with his assistant, Jen. I hadn't gone back to college. I wasn't able to see that Mike Papa was a dangerous fraud and a lowlife. Basically, he was trying to get his point across, even if it could hurt my feelings. All of it was more than I could handle. I was already feeling guilty about the whole thing and there was nothing I could do to change it. But he just kept railing. Finally, I found the courage to confront him.

"Let me fucking tell you something!" I shouted.

Dad sat back and looked at me. "Go ahead," he dared me, with his arms crossed.

"I can't take back anything I did," I said in a rage. "I live with this every single day of my life. If I could have done five years, I would have. My brother is in prison . . ." I was going to go on, but Dad interrupted.

"It makes me sick that my son is in prison. And it makes me sick that I couldn't make you see . . ."

This time I interrupted him. "You couldn't make us see, just like your parents couldn't make you see. I can't change what I did. I can only apologize to you. But you have to take responsibility for what you did, for being Sammy the Bull. If we were just Joe Schmo's kids, Gerard probably wouldn't have gotten jail time."

The release of my anger was really freeing me. "You thought when I was nineteen and you cooperated, I could just get up and move on with my life. You said you were always looking out for our benefit. You thought you always kept your life so separate and secret from us, but you didn't realize that we lived it, too. You don't know what it felt like to me when Uncle Eddie came over and told me to bring you cyanide and when people wouldn't let me into their houses because of you. I had to figure it out all on my own."

I couldn't leave out the part about how my own family, especially my baby Karina, could have been blown up by Peter Gotti and his hit team because of him. "We were minutes away from being blown away," I railed. "I can't move forward."

I left my father speechless. Finally he said, "You are right, you are one hundred percent right." He apologized.

It was a turning point for the two of us. It felt good. When I left the prison that day I felt like our relationship had been taken to a whole new level. I had grown up since our last encounter. I was in a more mature place, a place where I felt settled. I didn't leave as Sammy the Bull's daughter. I left as Karen Gravano, and I felt my father understood that, too. He was looking at me as an adult, separate from him. It had been such a tug-of-war to get here. I was thirty-one now, and finally had a clear understanding of me. I was on a path of my own choosing.

I was a single mother raising a nephew and a daughter all on my own, and I wanted to give them the best life I could. I decided that I was going to let go of all the anger and resentment I felt toward people who I blamed for wronging me. I had to be able to make my own mistakes and not blame anyone else for my decisions and actions.

Still, my father is a very valuable person to me. If I am going to do something, I run it by him. I like his opinion, even if I don't take the advice. I think Dad respects me as an adult now, too.

The time I spent in Arizona with my father, that year and a half when he was not in prison or witness protection, was important to me. Dad had explained a lot about his life in the mob, and it became clear why he made the decisions he did. But most important, I understood the way he loved his family. He used to say, "Every road you take in life blazes the path for those who follow." I finally understood what it meant.

I just wish Gerard and I had really understood what he was trying to say to us earlier. Perhaps my father wouldn't be doing twenty years in prison on drug charges? Maybe if my father had gotten it earlier in life himself, we all would have traveled a different path? Who knows? Maybe he would be dead.

I know that the decisions and choices that each of us has made has impacted us. But throughout all of our hardships, we have remained a family unit. We work every day to try and put it all behind us. Children of the Mafia live with scars and get terribly hurt. There's no getting out. But one thing I did learn is that if you have a loving and supportive family, it makes it easier to get through.

EPILOGUE

Five years after my arrest, I borrowed money from my grand-parents and bought The Body Wrap and Company, a health and wellness spa, from my boss. My dream of owning my own business and making enough money to support my family was coming true. My mother worked there with me. Shortly after we were arrested in 2000, my mother was forced to sell the restaurant and hand over the proceeds because of a lien the state of Arizona put on the business. They also put a lien on our property.

I loved having her at The Body Wrap. We offered every imaginable spa treatment, from wraps and peels to facials and body bronzing. About a year after I took ownership, I started to develop my own skin care line. I custom-made creams and products exclusively for my clients. The spa was so popular at its height that I had more than ten employees in the three-thousand-square-foot space.

Unfortunately, when the economy went bust in 2009, the spa suffered. Between the mortgage crisis and the recession, business started to drop off. People were no longer able to spend on luxury items such as facials and body treatments, keeping their money for the necessities. At that point, I started to realize I needed to branch out into other areas in order to support my daughter.

Around the same time the struggles at the spa began, I reconnected with Jennifer Graziano, my childhood friend from Staten Island. Jenn was always a go-getter. She was now running her own marketing company and working in the entertainment business. Jennifer already had a successful career working at Sony Music Entertainment and had decided to branch out on her own as well. We started meeting up in Los Angeles when she was there on business.

Jenn and I wanted to see if we could find a way to collaborate on something. We wanted to see if we could come up with a project that interested both of us. We talked about doing a scripted TV show about my "aromatherapy" days back in New York.

Jennifer also ran an idea by me about a reality show which is now known as *Mob Wives*, something she had talked to me about back in 2007 and had been working on ever since. She had grown up in that world and now realized the cast members had been right under her nose for most of her life—Drita, Renee, and me.

When Jennifer first sprung the idea on me, I was not so open to it. I had always been so private about my personal life, especially when it came to the lifestyle I had grown up in. I felt like reality TV was not the place for me to open up. But after a couple of conversations, I saw Jennifer's vision. She did not want to focus so much on the mob, but more on the lifestyle and its effect on the family, both positive and negative. After casting Drita, Renee, and me, Jenn decided she needed a fourth woman. Renee suggested her friend Carla Facciolo, who was married to a guy in prison and who had connections through her family to this lifestyle. Although Drita had absolutely no mob ties, Jenn thought her character would be good for television.

By April of 2010, I decided to close the spa. Financially, I couldn't ride the wave until the recession was over. And now I had other interests going on. I had reached a point in my life where I had fully come to terms with everything that had happened to me, and was ready to write my story, as well as let America in on who I am as a person now through my participation in *Mob Wives*.

When the show was first bought by VH1, the other girls had reservations about working with me: Renee because she worried about what her father would say; Carla because she cared about what other people would think about her; and Drita because she was concerned about the world knowing that she and I were friends and she married my ex-boyfriend.

Jennifer did not let that get in the way of her vision. She felt that when all four of us got together, we each brought something to the show. I was bringing the biggest last name in the mob because of who my father was. Renee was bringing a larger than life personality, and Jennifer always knew that when her sister made her TV debut, she was going to be a star. Drita was a character, as was Carla.

I was okay with being on the show with everyone. I felt that we were all women in the same situation, and pretty much all of us were single moms raising our kids. I am not going to lie, I felt uncomfortable when we began filming season one because of everything that was brought back up about my father. I have always been a very private person, and I felt exposed. After a couple of days of filming, I realized that this was something I chose to do, and I began to see the bigger picture. It was rewarding for me coming back to New York. When I left Staten Island for Arizona, a part of me had wanted to stay. Now, I was coming back with a fuller understanding of who I was.

After a while, Renee and I moved past our issues, and she and I have been building a bond and a true friendship. As for Drita, I realized that we were never really true friends, and I am okay with that. It was great to be back and reconnect with Jennifer. Now I'm on the show with Ramona Rizzo, the newest cast member, whom I consider family.

Ramona has been a lifelong friend, she understands me, and having her on the show has added a whole unique twist. It feels good to have someone who is loyal. Having Ramona on the show brings me back to memories of the lifestyle we grew up in. We were apart for a while. She was married and raising four kids, and I was in Arizona dealing with my life. When she and I came together for season two, it was like we hadn't skipped a beat.

In season two, we focused more on the five women, our stories, and our businesses. I have always been a businesswoman, so I was excited to share that side of myself with our viewers. It was also exciting to bring the show to an international audience and to have people outside of the United States hearing our stories.

The hardest part for me is being away from Karina. She is

in Arizona with my mother. I am so thankful for my mother. She has always co-parented Karina with me, and she continues to do so today. My daughter is also spending time with her father and I think it is really good. She and Dave are rebuilding their relationship, and that is important.

I have a lot going on in New York. I am in the process of getting back into the spa business, and have decided to go back to developing my skin care line. That has been something I have always wanted to do, and when I decide to do something, I feel like I need to accomplish it.

My mother and brother are in Arizona. Gerard was released from prison on January 19, 2009, and he has been working as a chef. He is actually in the process of creating his own line of sauces from recipes that he gathered growing up. The name of the company is The Gravanos, and Gerard is selling the products through our family website, thegravanos.com.

My father is still in prison, serving the remainder of his nineteen-year sentence on the Arizona drug charges. His agreeing to accept a plea deal in that case was very hard for me to deal with, so I decided to revisit that case, and I have uncovered new information that I believe proves that my father had minimal involvement in the Ecstasy ring, and that his only crime was loaning my brother and Mike Papa money. I don't know where my investigation is going to lead, but with an attorney on board, I feel that this is something I need to shed light on. From what I have uncovered so far, I believe that it is going to be explosive.

My father and I speak regularly. He is not a hundred percent on board with the content of *Mob Wives*, but he understands why I am doing the show and he supports me in my decision. I have talked with him about the book and, like everyone else,

245

he is anxious to read it. He is there for me as a friend. Even if he doesn't agree with me completely, it does not affect our relationship. Nothing will ever affect that. He is my father and I love him.

He is fighting hard to keep his health, and he works out every day. He will never be able to grow his hair back, but his mental state is good. Physically, his color has come back, he is fit and he has gained some weight. For that, I am grateful.

One thing I realized was that if I had to do it all over again, I would not change a thing. Everything that happened to my family is what made us who we are today. I just wish my father could be with his grandkids. I wish he could see Nicholas play baseball. Nicholas is so good that he has been selected to play on a pre-Olympic team. I wish he could come and see Karina play volleyball. I wish he could be a part of their lives. But we do the best we can with phone calls and an occasional visit. And I try and make him a part of it all by being here on the outside.

When I left New York in 1998, I was in a vulnerable state. I was confused and still looking for answers. Now that I am back, I feel like I have found those answers. Old friends have welcomed me home, and even some of my father's old friends have come out of the woodwork to reconnect with me. It's like my life has come full circle.

Even with Aunt Fran and Uncle Eddie, I have moved past all the anger and hurt and have made amends. One day, when I was in the spa in Arizona, Aunt Fran's telephone number popped into my head and I just dialed it. She thought I was calling to tell her that something had happened to my father. I said that he was fine, and that I wanted to call her and start to rebuild our relationship.

Now when we talk, we don't bring up the past, we focus on the present and the future. It is the same way with my uncle Eddie. Uncle Eddie is still in prison, and I have come to a place of forgiveness. He is no different from my father. He made his mistakes just like my father did and I forgave my father, so why wouldn't I forgive him?

We have to break the cycle for our kids. We don't want to keep passing this legacy down from generation to generation. That is what we have done. One thing I have learned is that you can't choose your family. I wouldn't change mine. I am completely happy with them. I love them, and I always will.